By the same author:

WELL MET IN MADRID

WELL MET IN MADRID

Archibald Lyall

De Madrid al cielo y en el cielo
una ventanilla para ver Madrid

Illustrated by
Rafael Alvarez Ortega

PUTNAM
42 GREAT RUSSELL STREET
LONDON WCI

Printed in Great Britain by
The Camelot Press Ltd., London and Southampton

As a bullfighter throws his hat upon the sand when he dedicates his bull to the public, so I dedicate my book to the *gatos*, the gay, gallant, warmhearted, witty people of Madrid.

CONTENTS

CHAPTER ONE

Angel's Eye View

The local saying quoted on the title-page embodies the ambition of every good *gato*—'From Madrid to Heaven, and in Heaven a little window from which to look at Madrid.'

Until very recently he could not see Madrid from Heaven and return, should he wish (as many a true Madrileño might), to Madrid, but now he can get a very fair preview by taking the lift to the restaurant-café on the twenty-sixth floor of the Edificio España in the Plaza de España. There he will see all Madrid spread out at his feet. In the distance, across the valley of the Manzanares, are the scattered ilex, elms and pinewoods of the Casa del Campo, the Richmond Park of Madrid; beyond it are the wide bare uplands of Castile, and away to the left the statue-crowned hill of the Cerro de los Angeles, which is reckoned to be the exact geographical centre of the great Peninsula; on the horizon the blue Castilian sky is cut by the ridges of the Sierra de Guadarrama, white in the winter months with snow.

Beneath him lies Madrid, or, as it used often to be called, *los Madriles*, for there are several distinct Madrids. At his feet, close-packed above the narrow streets which look from here like fine cracks in a dried-up field, are the low-pitched, tawny, curly-tiled roofs and the grey-brown, peeling stucco walls of eighteenth-century Madrid. Beyond are the new residential districts, the Barrios Altos, built between fifty and a hundred years ago on either side of the Paseo de la Castellana.

Against the dark trees of the Retiro Park the white tower of the Central Post Office stands out like a bad pastiche of Ely Cathedral (*Nuestra Señora de las Comunicaciones*, as the Madrileño wits promptly christened it) and to its left is the square red block of the Buenavista Palace, which once belonged to Goya's friend, the Duchess of Alba, and is now the War Office.

Southward beyond the high concrete buildings, the Telefónica tower and the neon-signs of the Gran Vía, a canyon gashed through the heart of the old town in the earlier decades of the century, lies the Madrid of the Golden Age, where the curious Central-European-looking spires which mark such buildings as the Ayuntamiento, the Panadería in the Plaza Mayor, and the Palace of Santa Cruz, crowd each other as in a mediaeval German town, and remind us that this was the so-called 'Austrian' period. In the distance loom the great new blocks of workers' dwellings, beyond the river on the Andalusia highway.

On the other side of our Madrileño observer are the new blocks of flats in the Rosales and Argüelles quarters and beyond them the great red palaces of the University City. All these were in the front line during the Civil War and were almost totally destroyed; in this direction he is looking at nothing which has not been built or rebuilt in the last twenty years. Turning on his heel further round to the north and east he will see the

San Francisco

semicircle of huge white and red skyscraper blocks spring-ing up like a miniature cave-dwelt Sierra all round the fringes of the town at Cuatro Caminos, Chamartín, La Guindalera, Prosperidad, El Barrio de la Concep-ción, and the new quarter beyond the Retiro—the high brick and concrete rampart which is the newest of all *los Madriles*.

The City which is not a City

Of all great European capitals, Madrid is the one which most bristles with paradoxes and offers the most contrasts and inconsistencies. It is at once the least Spanish and the most Spanish town in the Peninsula—the least Spanish because it is the most modernised and international, and the most Spanish because, perhaps on account of its four centuries as a sort of 'Washington, D.C.' and of the mixed population which has flowed into it from the various regions of Spain, it is a synthesis of them all. In Barcelona one is all the time aware of being in Catalonia, and in Seville one could be nowhere except in Andalusia, but Madrid is not particularly Castilian in the sense that the smaller cities of Castile are Castilian. It is Spanish, and that is all.

The country which a sound instinct tells us is the oldest in Western Europe (even if the dry dates of history support the unexpected claims of such dark horses as Denmark and San Marino) has a capital which hardly existed a thousand years ago and was still little more than a village five hundred years later. (In 1530 it had only three thousand inhabitants, according to Fernández de

Oviedo.) It is a babe-in-arms compared with Paris, London or half a dozen cities in Castile itself.

For three centuries the capital of the largest empire the world had ever seen, Madrid, has never been a 'city' and even now ranks only as a 'town'. (I have travelled on two ships of the Trasmediterranea Line: one was called *La Ciudad de Ibiza* and the other *La Villa de Madrid*.) It only became the capital of Spain because Philip II fixed his court here and made it *La Corte*—which is still its official designation. Indeed, it would be interesting to learn from some constitutional lawyer whether Spain legally had any capital at all after the abolition of the Monarchy, and therefore of the Court, in 1931. Possibly, Spain being theoretically a monarchy once more, Madrid became the capital again only in 1950, when it incorporated within its boundaries El Pardo, where the Chief of State resides.

Until the Concordat of 1851 the seat of the Most Catholic Kings and the capital of the most intensely Catholic country in Europe was without a cathedral. It still has only a temporary one, and even now it shares a bishop with Alcalá de Henares, rather like Bath and Wells. Nor did the new diocese start auspiciously; no bishop was appointed for a number of years, and the first of them, D. Narciso Martínez, was assassinated by a priest as he entered San Isidro, the great Jesuit church which had been named as cathedral, to celebrate Mass on Palm Sunday, 1886.

While every other inland capital in Western Europe has developed in all directions from a central kernel, Madrid alone, the one which lies furthest from the sea, has developed only in a half-circle, for all the world like a seaport town. The original nucleus was built on the brow of a steep and wide ravine which has ever since acted like a waterfront to prevent the city (for such we must, if we are not to fall into pedantry, call it) from spreading to the west. Only in 1948 did the Carabancheles, the two villages just beyond the river, become part of Madrid, either physically or administratively.

I have lived in half a dozen foreign capitals and there is no city I know harder to get the feel of than Madrid. Several decades ago Ramón Gómez de la Serna, the well-known chronicler of the capital, wrote that '*Madrid es la capital del mundo mas difícil de comprender*'. This is even truer today, for it is at present in a state of transition or tension, where the eighteenth century vigorously holds its own against a fierce onslaught of modernisation or, as it is locally called, 'americanisation'. One finds oneself hoping that, if 'americanisation' is really the irresistible force it sometimes seems to be, it may at last have come up against an immovable object in Spain.

The city which boasts of the two tallest skyscrapers in Europe is on the main route along which the great flocks of sheep traditionally move between the pastures of Northern Spain in the summer and Southern Spain in the winter; every spring millions of sheep are driven north and every autumn millions are driven south, past the banks and the skyscrapers, along the whole length of the Calle de Alcalá, the main street of the city. Two stones incised with the word '*Canada*' near the Puerta de Alcalá, which marked it as an official sheep track, were only removed three or four years ago.

Civil Guards in shiny, black winged hats like Samurai stroll past neon-lit cocktail bars, and night-watchmen with their holly-staves must be summoned with hand-claps to unlock the doors of great modern buildings of plate-glass and chromium. Once (though admittedly it was thirty years ago) I even saw a pilgrim, hung round with scallop-shells, unconcernedly striding with his staff up the Gran Vía past the Telefónica skyscraper; he was doubtless on his way back from Santiago de Compostela, for cockleshells were the emblem of St. James (whence the *Coquille St. Jacques* of West End restaurants). Nowhere else in Western Europe are the old and the new so com-mingled. To see such exciting juxtapositions one must cross the Mediterranean or the Dardanelles, and even there, in contrast to Madrid, it is generally a cheap, shoddy new rubbing elbows with a pretty moth-eaten, broken-down old.

The Childhood of Madrid

In Europe at any rate, the present is always rooted in the past. A city is an organic, living growth, and it is not possible to understand it without some idea of its history, or, to employ the modern monosyllables fashionable today, one must find out how it got to be the way it is before one can start to make sense of it. Fortunately for the reader who tends to be bored by the biography of a city, Madrid has a life-span only a quarter the length of, say, Rome or Stambul.

A thousand years ago, where the Royal Palace stands today, a small Moorish castle called Madjrit crowned the eastern bluff above the Manzanares valley (what would have been called a *wadi* when this part of Spain still belonged to the Arabs and is now called a *barranco*). It was a distant outwork of the defence system of the Moorish capital, Toledo, which was then beginning to feel itself menaced by the southward advance of the Christian kings from Old Castile. Under the cover of its walls a small Moslem village huddled on the little hill where now is the church of San Nicolás. Madjrit was captured by Alfonso XI of Castile in 1085—nineteen years after Duke William of Normandy conquered England—and from then on it began slowly to grow until by the end of the fifteenth century the walls had expanded south-eastward to what are still called the Puerta de Moros and the Puerta de Cebada and halfway down the Calle Mayor—then, as now, the main artery of Old Madrid, leading from the Palace 'inland' from the Manzanares cliff-edge and continuing on to Alcalá de Henares.

The quarter east and south of the Palace on both sides of the Calle de Segovia and of the Calle Mayor as far as the Plaza de los Herradores, just short of the Plaza Mayor, constituted mediaeval Madrid. To wander in its narrow twisting streets and quiet tree-shaded *plazuelas* is a pleasure which most foreign visitors and many Madrileños have never discovered, but the scutcheoned houses of long-dead noblemen and the façades of the baroque churches all date from the 'Austrian' period, the sixteenth and seventeenth centuries when the Habsburgs were the Kings of Spain. Of mediaeval Madrid nothing is left which is not very much restored or reconstructed, such as the Mudéjar towers of San Nicolás and San Pedro el Viejo, built in the Moorish style for Christian masters by Moslem artisans, and, of secular architecture, only parts of the Torre de los Lujanes and the house next door in the Plaza de la Villa.

It is the Torre de los Lujanes that tradition has fixed on as the first place of imprisonment of Francis I of France after his defeat at Pavia. The Spaniards, who have had more than one French King foisted upon them, have never forgotten the time they captured a King of France in open battle, and four centuries later they eat a dish of salt cod fried in oil called *Los Soldaditos de Pavía*, The Little Soldiers of Pavia, from its supposed resemblance to the yellow tunics of the old Regiment of Hussars of Pavia. Francis' magnificent campaigning tent, captured on the battlefield, is still displayed like a trophy in the Armoury of the Palace.

Madrid of the Renaissance

The Kings of Castile were constantly moving about their dominions, and their capital was wherever the court happened to find itself at the moment. The most favoured cities were Valladolid, Toledo, Burgos, Segovia and Seville, but sometimes the court was pitched (for that is the only possible word) at Madrid or some other small town. The first King who came to live for any length of time in the Alcázar at Madrid was Charles I, better known as the Holy Roman Emperor Charles V, who ruled not only Spain but Austria, Flanders, the Netherlands, Burgundy, two-thirds of Italy and vast unexplored and hardly imagined territories in the Americas. The sad, tired face of the most powerful monarch the world had known since Diocletian can be seen in Titian's great portraits in the Prado. Finding the dry air good for his 'gout', a generic term which included arthritis, rheumatism and other less mentionable maladies, he settled down in Madrid for several years until, weary and disillusioned, he followed Diocletian's example, laid down all his heavy titles and retired to die in the Monastery of Yuste in Estremadura.

The first king to fix his Court permanently at Madrid was Charles' son, Philip II, who married an unhappy Queen of England, Mary Tudor, and after her death launched the Great Armada against her sister in an attempt to regain his lost kingdom. His only comment when they brought him the news of the disaster was: 'Thank God I have the money to build another navy!'

It is said that in those days Madrid was surrounded by forests, which were cut down to provide timber for the new buildings of the city. It may well be so, but why exactly the new capital was fixed in this little town out on the wind-bitten, sun-baked steppes remains a puzzle to which everyone will give a different answer. Certainly there were a number of excellent reasons why it should be in this part of Castile. One was the dry, sharp air, for Philip was an even sicklier man than his father; another was its central position and the consequent ease of communications with all parts of the Peninsula; yet a third, its relative detachment from the political jealousies of 'the Spains', still only recently united.

But, after all, the 'forests' can have been little more than the scraggy ilex-groves of the Casa del Campo, the air is much the same all over the plateau of Castile, and a matter of a few miles one way or another makes no difference in a country the size of Spain. There was already an ancient and flourishing city, for centuries the capital of Gothic, Moorish and Castilian kings, only forty miles away at Toledo. If it was argued, no doubt with reason, that Toledo was for physical reasons incapable of being expanded and developed into a modern capital and that it was so ineradicably permeated with Arab and Jewish influences that an Operation Ankara was necessary, then the obvious choice for a new capital would seem to have been the sheltered, shady, fertile, well-watered oasis of Aranjuez (which the late General O'Duffy used to call 'Orange Juice') a few miles away on the Tagus, where there already existed a palace which Ferdinand and Isabella had taken from the Grand Master of the Knights of Santiago and made into a royal residence. It is said that Philip picked on Madrid as the easiest place from which to supervise the building of his pet project, the Monastery-Palace-Mausoleum of the Escorial. That again may well be so, but it took the sick man a week to travel in a carrying-chair from Madrid to the Escorial; why did he not build his new city at El Escorial itself?

Be that as it may, Madrid, from being a tiny provincial town with a royal hunting-lodge, became the Ankara-cum-Canberra of Spain and has remained the capital ever since. For a brief period Philip III tried to transfer it to Valladolid, only to be so blocked by the many vested interests which in forty years had grown up in Madrid that he soon had to move back again. The Duke of Lerma bought an estate and built himself a palace on the site of the present Palace Hotel (which takes its name from it) out of the gold given him by the grateful people of Madrid for his part in engineering the return.

From then on the history of Madrid is mainly the history of its steady expansion to the east, north and south, and of the social and architectural changes which accompanied the different stages. Madrid has occasionally leapt into the forefront of events in such sudden outbursts of violence, heroism and cruelty as the rising of the unarmed populace against the French troops on May 2nd, 1808 (Goya's famous *Dos de Mayo*), which was comparable in many ways with the Budapest rising of October 1956 and was perhaps the original bacillus to enter and eventually to destroy the all-powerful system of Napoleon, and the revolution, counter-revolution and siege of Madrid from 1936-9, still fresh in the memories of many who are yet young. But such epic interludes have proved mere passing interruptions to the steady, peaceful development of the city. They resulted in changes to its mode of life lasting, it is undeniable, but perhaps less far-reaching and revolutionary than might have been imagined by many contemporary observers.

CHAPTER TWO

Los Madriles

Madrid is a conglomeration of townships built on to each other in different centuries and in different styles of architecture, generally after long periods of comparative inactivity. In the words of the great novelist of nineteenth-century Madrid, Benito Pérez Galdós, the urbanisation of Madrid has progressed in a series of *brusquedades*. One such abrupt leap occurred in the reign of Charles III. The earlier buildings of Madrid, even the churches and the palaces, had been built of mud, adobe or at best of brick, with wooden floors and ceilings, and sometimes with elaborately carved stone portals stuck on to them like poultices, as Ribera's lovely portals had been plastered on only forty years before.

Now the typically eighteenth-century monarch decided the time had come for the rather shoddy capital of his great empire to have fine stone buildings like Paris and Rome, and to this end he employed a trio of brilliant architects who in some twenty years, roughly speaking in the 1770's and '80's, transformed the face of Madrid with a series of public buildings and monuments in the neo-classical style known after their patron as *carloterceristo*. These three men were Sabatini, Ventura Rodríguez and Villanueva. Another

Madrid from

ALVAREZ ORTEGA.

del Camp

brusquedad was taken when the Salamanca Quarter was begun in 1872; a third, only a short time later when the *Barrios Altos* spread north and east from Chamberí; and yet a fourth after the Civil War when, as a result of the new government's policy of centralisation, Madrid replaced Barcelona as the commercial capital of Spain.

At the beginning of the present century the *villa* had about a quarter of a million people. Now it has overhauled Barcelona and only by a couple of months been beaten by Rome in the race to reach the two million mark. (The two millionth citizen of Madrid, Isabel Ana Sainz de Cueto y Torres, was born at half past six on the morning of July 3rd, 1959.) In the olden days it could have none but small local industries owing to lack of water and fuel. Now heavy industry, near Barajas, in Chamartín and out along the Andalusia Highway, is beginning to encircle the city. Some of the increase in population has been achieved by clever juggling with boundaries. Between 1948 and 1950 the municipal area was almost decupled by the inclusion of the villages of Chamartín, the two Carabancheles, Aravaca, Barajas, Canillas, Hortaleza, Fuencarral, El Pardo, Vallecas and Vicálvaro. All the same, most of the increase is genuine. It is estimated that nearly half the population were born in Toledo, Guadalajara and the other provinces of the Central Plateau, and there are about a hundred thousand natives of the Northern Coast. There are fewer immigrants from the east and south, where Barcelona, Valencia and Seville act as magnets for the local peasantry.

Madrid is popularly divided into three sections. The *Barrios Centrales* or Central Quarters need no explanation; the *Barrios Bajos* are in fact working-class districts but take their name of the Low Quarters because they comprise the districts which slope down to the river southward from the Plaza Mayor and the Plaza de Tirso de Molina. The *Barrios Altos*, the newer suburbs which have sprung up to the north and north-east, are so called not because they are mostly well-to-do quarters but because they occupy the high ground. For example, the reservoir at Cuatro Caminos is three hundred feet above the level of the Delicias Station.

The Axis of Madrid

Madrid has always tended to spread along a single main axis, largely no doubt because of the Manzanares barrier to the west. The first was along the road 'inland' from the Alcázar de los Reyes, as the Palace was still known, which continued to the ancient University city of Alcalá de Henares, the birthplace of Cervantes and of our Catherine of Aragon, and on across the great steppelands to Guadalajara, Saragossa and Barcelona. In the sixteenth century the city expanded eastward as far as the Puerta del Sol, which may have been called the Sun Gate because it faced the rising sun, but which more probably took the name which Madrid shares with Cuzco and Perugia because the fort, built to protect the Guadalajara Gate at the time of the Comunero War, had a carved sun on its wall. *Post hoc* or *propter hoc?*

For centuries this was the centre of Madrid life and gossip, the *Mentidero* or Lie Exchange (which was on the terrace of San Felipe el Real), the magnet for the diversions and taverns, and the starting place not only of all the coach and postal services of Spain but of the innumerable riots and revolutions. The Puerta del Sol had the first gas lamp in Spain in 1830, the first public urinal in 1863, the first mule tram in 1871, the first electric light in 1875 and the first electric tram in 1879. When in 1856 its reconstruction was decreed, a revolution promptly broke out and brought down the Government of Spain. We shall be returning to it later. One always does in Madrid.

From the Puerta del Sol the principal axis of the expanding city pushed ahead along the Calle de Alcalá, as the Calle Mayor was from this point onwards to be called. The Alcalá stretches, wide and straight for miles, until out beyond the bullring it becomes the Aragon Highway. But as far as modish Madrid was concerned it came to an end at the Plaza de Cibeles where it crossed the great avenue which runs from Atocha, where the southern slums begin, up to the remote northern limits of the city. To the south were the fashionable promenades of the Salón del Prado and the Paseo del Prado; on the square where they meet the two great international hotels, the Ritz and the Palace, were built facing each other in 1910, as though to set the stamp upon the supersession of the Puerta del Sol, where the old Hotel de Paris had so long reigned supreme.

Then instead of turning south, as it seemed it was going to do, at the Plaza de Cibeles, or continuing straight on to the Retiro and the Salamanca Quarter, the axis of fashion shied abruptly like a nervous bull leftward and northward up the Paseo de los Recoletos and the Paseo de la Castellana, and it is there that the latest luxury flats and hotels of the 1950's, such as the Castellana

Hilton, the Fénix and the Savoy, are now replacing the old
nineteenth-century mansions and gardens of the nobility.

Old Madrid

Except for the bizarre roof of San Pedro el Viejo, Saint
Peter the Old, there is hardly anything left of fifteenth-
century Madrid. The centre of the town was the Straw
Market, the square now called the Plaza de Comillas,
where Ferdinand and Isabella stayed in the Palace of Don
Pedro Lasso de la Vega and where Cardinal Cisneros
overawed the rebellious nobles of Castile. Its sole attraction now is the Capilla del Obispo, the Bishop's Chapel
which contains the only good pieces of Renaissance
sculpture in Madrid, Francisco Giralta's great *reredos* and
the tomb of the Vargas family. This district became the
Morería or Moorish quarter—which is why the smart
modern flamenco restaurant above at Las Vistillas is
named the Corral de la Morería.

From Las Vistillas, the Little Views, and the viaduct
over the Calle de Segovia, which the poet Emilio
Carrère called Suicide's Balcony, there is a magnificent
view over the great wide country to the west. Indeed,
Madrid, built as it is on a series of sandy bluffs overlooking
the Manzanares valley, makes a somewhat thin claim to
be built on seven hills like Rome, Lisbon and Stambul.
Often one turns a corner in the busy centre of the city
and comes with sudden delight upon a view of the open
country down a steeply sloping street. But Las Vistillas
is still the best place to see those breath-taking Castilian
sunsets.

On the Cuesta de la Vega, beside the Viaduct, the new Cathedral of Santa María de Almudena is being erected in a more than Fabian fashion. The plans were approved in 1879 and work was begun twenty years later. So far only the crypt is completed, which is not so surprising when one considers that for many years its annual budget was restricted to a hundred thousand pesetas, nor so regrettable when one considers also the change of taste since the time of the original architect, the Marqués de Cubas, who designed an enormous and ornate building in German Gothic, which would have entirely dwarfed the Royal Palace.

Meanwhile the great Jesuit Collegiate Church of San Isidro, half-destroyed in 1936, still serves as a temporary cathedral. None of the baroque churches of Madrid are of much interest inside. What little they contained was mostly looted or burned by the mob in 1936, although San Francisco El Grande, San Antonio and San Bernardo still possess a Goya apiece and San Ginés an El Greco. There is, incidentally, a fine El Greco *Annunciation* in the Banco de Urquijo in the Calle de Alcalá. You have only to walk into the Bank and up the stairs to find it hanging on the left-hand side of the first-floor corridor.

The Palace

Next door to the Cathedral is the former Royal Palace. It is worth a visit for the magnificent Tiepolo ceiling in the throne-room and for the curious Gasparini Room, a piece of *chinoiserie* whose walls and ceilings are entirely composed of painted flowers and figures in porcelain

Palacio Real

relief. But, except for four Goya portraits and two small Velázquez's, nearly all the pictures from Philip IV's great collection have been moved to the Prado. The Moorish Alcázar, reconstructed in the turreted 'Austrian' manner and burned down on Christmas Eve 1734, was rebuilt in the classical style by Philip V. He called on Juvara for the original plans, but the great architect who created modern Turin died before he could come to Madrid, and the present palace is the work of his compatriot Sacchetti.

Between the Palace and the Cathedral-to-be-or-not-to-be is the west parade ground where to the imperious blare of trumpets the armies of the Great Captain and the other Spanish generals used to form up and march away to the conquest of Europe. On the western side of this great dusty square is the Armoury, a collection unrivalled in Europe, which contains all the chased and inlaid parade and tournament armour of Charles V. There is the original suit of armour which the Emperor wore at the Battle of Mühlberg and which Titian painted in his great equestrian portrait in the Prado. His armour was all made from a mould of himself which was made in Toledo in 1525 and taken back to Augsburg by the greatest armourer of the age, Koloman Kolmann. There is armour here not only for kings, for knights and for horses (twenty of them), but even the suit made for Don Balthasar Carlos, the pathetic child whom Velázquez painted, and a suit of chain mail and a 'tin hat' for a favourite greyhound.

There are relics of mediaeval conquerors such as St. Ferdinand and Jaime I, the Moorish standard taken at the great battle of Las Navas de Tolosa, which sealed the fate of Moslem Spain in 1212, Turkish trophies from Lepanto,

Francis I's war-tent from Pavia, the swords of Cortes and of Pizarro, of Ferdinand and Isabella and of Don John of Austria, down to the Duke of Wellington. Everywhere there are relics of Charles V—'la bomba atomica' as the guide calls him to show that, though forced to spend his days among all this obsolete armament, he at least keeps up with the times.

Many weapons are missing from the original collection but they were put to a good use when Madrid rose against the French on May 2nd, 1808 (and even old Goya, Francophile though he was, sniped at the Mamelukes from a fourth-floor window of the Puerta del Sol). The rebels helped themselves, it is said, to three hundred swords and many other weapons. One wonders what would have happened if only Madrid had possessed an armoury like that of the Zeughaus in Graz, which even today can arm and equip twenty thousand halberdiers and pikemen from its stocks at half an hour's notice. Napoleon might have been driven from Spain in 1808 and many a British regiment done out of half a dozen cherished battle honours. No Badajoz, no Salamanca, no Talavera, no Albuera, no Vitoria, no Pamplona.

It is interesting to observe how closely the armour followed the civilian fashions of the day, and how the foot-style changed when pointed shoes were replaced by square toes; the tight-waisted cuirass copied the doublet, and the lamboys or petticoat mimicked puffed-out trunk-hose. (The slashing seems to have been left to the enemy.) Similar greaves and cuisses to those in the Armoury are still worn by the picadors every Sunday in the Madrid bullring.

In all the world there are only about forty helmets

B

which model faces and quite a few of them are here in
the Madrid Armoury. Some are 'grotesques' and others
are animal heads; the most interesting of all is Charles V's
own portrait, his 'mask helmet' as the Spaniards call it.
This kind of embossed and damascened metalwork is as
fine a craft as the goldsmith's, and one feels that Ben-
venuto Cellini himself would not have disdained it.

When you leave the Armoury look over the balcony
at the Campo del Moro sloping steeply down from the
Palace like the Villa d'Este at Tivoli. It used to be the
private garden of the Spanish kings. I have seen it look
fantastically like a Chinese print when on a damp
December day the ragged black cedar- and pine-tops rose
like spectres out of a dense white mist. It is called the
Moor's Field because Ali Ben Yusuf the Almoravide
pitched his camp there when he besieged the castle of
Madrid in the twelfth century. That was not the last time
that the Alcázar has been in the front line or faced the
Moors, for the numerous punctures in the armour which
contemporary weapons could not dent were made by
shellfire during the Civil War of 1936-9.

The Square of the Orient

In front of the Palace, on the western cliff-edge of
Madrid, is the inappositely named Plaza de Oriente. It
was created by Napoleon's brother, King Joseph Bonaparte, who pulled down several convents, a church, a
library and fifty-six houses to clear the space. It is a very
peaceful place, with some of those magnificent trees,
planes, cedars and deodars, which Madrid is, in her rather

Jardín de Oriente

indolent fashion, capable of producing when she chooses to do so. It is a favourite haunt of nursemaids and children. The children vainly hunt the croaking frogs in the fountains and the pretty *chachas* are equally vainly hunted by idle soldiers off duty, for where there are nursemaids there will always be soldiers. In the summer the Restaurant Wamba transplants its kitchens and tables and chairs from the Calle de Bola to the Plaza, and one can eat very agreeably beneath the trees and catch any errant breeze that may be blowing.

In the square a number of pedestals and inscriptions commemorate long-forgotten Gothic kings. There must be scores of these statues in all, for many others are in the Sabatini Gardens nearby and in the Parterre of the Retiro Park, where their heads rear snake-like out of the tree-tops like Alice in Wonderland, and where the inscriptions add anonymity to immortality by hiding in the shrubbery which veils their lower limbs. These statues were originally designed to line the roof of Philip V's new palace, Italian fashion, but very prudently they were never put up there for fear that they might prove too heavy and pull the building down. There is a more or less inexhaustible supply of (usually very short-lived and bloody-ended) Spanish monarchs, Visigothic, Asturian, Castilian, Aragonese, Leonese and Navarrese, so that both the Plaza de Oriente and the Retiro seem to be stocked for eternity.

The statue of Philip IV in the middle of the Square is the work of the Florentine sculptor, Pietro Tacca, who never saw the king but who was sent two portraits by Velázquez, one half-length and one equestrian, to serve as his model. He did a good job artistically, but it is easier to make a horse cavort on canvas than in bronze, and to solve the technical problems no less a person than Galileo himself had to be called in. The result of the sage's calculations is to be seen in the hind legs and the great tail (always the pride of Spanish steeds, or at least of their masters) which supports the eighteen thousand pounds of rearing bronze like a tree trunk.

The Austrian Quarter

The so-called 'Austrian' quarter, on both sides of the Calle Mayor, consisted mainly of the mud-and-timber houses of the residents, if not attracted at least attached, to King Philip's new little capital. They were mostly small and mean, the so-called *casas de malicia*, put up, with that inbred Spanish instinct to ride round the law, for the express purpose of countering the royal edict that all houses above a certain size must lodge one or more officials of the Court. (No fewer than thirty-five of them were pulled down to build the Casa de Correos, later the Gobernación and now the Seguridad in the Puerta del Sol—and, as we have seen, fifty-six to clear the Plaza de Oriente.) A third of the area of Madrid was covered by churches and convents. Philip II founded seventeen, Philip III fourteen and Philip IV, who also left thirty natural children, seventeen. They were mostly, like the other public buildings, built in Philip II's *estilo desornamentado*, of which the Escorial is the best-known example, and by which he replaced the gay light Isabelline style then in vogue. Can the replacement of the First Spanish Renaissance style by the Second be connected with the introduction of syphilis into Europe? Were 'the Spanish evil' and the Counter-Reformation jointly responsible for the destruction of joy in Spanish architecture?

The ideal of Philip's architects, Juan Bautista de Toledo and Juan de Herrera, was a plain, unadorned surface flanked by the queer little slate-tiled steeples, splayed out below like ballet-dancers' skirts, so characteristic of the village churches all over New Castile to this day. If we contemplate the old University at Alcalá de Henares or the Church of San Juan de los Reyes at Toledo, we can see how much Madrid has lost through the austere monarch's contempt for the delightful style of the First Spanish Renaissance.

Few public buildings of the 'Second Renaissance' period now survive; among them are Gómez de Mora's *Ayuntamiento* and Crescenzi's Palacio de Santa Cruz, now the Foreign Office and formerly the Court Prison where George Borrow was locked up for selling bibles. There are none, alas, of the Isabelline or plateresque style.

Many of the convents were pulled down by a much hated, absurd, but still pathetic and not entirely unlovable Corsican peasant called Joseph Bonaparte who created so many new squares that his derisive and unappreciative subjects nicknamed him *El Rey Plazuelas*. Previously Madrid had been thickly built up and there were hardly any breaks among the houses and convents except for the little triangular village greens where two streets happened to cut into each other at an acute angle. They survive today in the Plaza de las Cortes and in the more plebeian Lavapiés. There is a typical example in London in front of the Victoria and Albert Museum.

It was left to nature who, after all, created the Grand

Canyon of Colorado, to create the Plaza de Callao, now one of the main city centres, when in 1860 a block of buildings folded up and collapsed between the Calle de los Preciados and the Calle de Carmen. But King Joseph, nicknamed also *Pepe Botella* or Joe Bottle, in addition to clearing the Plaza de Oriente, played Old Harry (if 'playing Old Harry' means following the example of Henry VIII) among the convents; the Plaza de Santa Ana was once St. Theresa's Convent of the Carmelites of St. Anne and the adjoining Plaza del Angel the Monastery of St. Philip Neri. The market of Los Mostenses is on the site of the Convent of the Premostratensians and those of Carmen and of San Ildefonso of the convents of the same names; the Plaza de Cristino Martos, the Plaza de San Miguel, the Plaza de San Martín, the Plaza de Tirso de Molina and the Plaza del Rey are other squares made by Joseph out of convent sites.

The Rain in Spain

The Tagus Basin shares one misfortune with England in that the prevailing winds blow either cold and dry from the north-east or warm and damp from the south-west. All the winds except the southerly cross the mountain-tops, and more especially the Sierra de Guadarrama which girdles Madrid on the north. That is why Argüelles and the University City are reputed to be the coldest (or, if you prefer, the coolest) quarters of the town, and the sheltered Cibeles and Atocha quarters the warmest. Anyone coming to Madrid, by the way, should be fore-warned that the spring has the reputation of being the rainy season—what the Spaniards call *las aguas de mayo*, 'the May waters'. Next to May, the two pluvious peaks are February and November. It seldom rains in the summer, except for sudden torrential thunderstorms, generally in the evening.

When the woodlands which surrounded the old hunting lodge were cut down to build the new capital, the birds went away, the streams disappeared, the soil became barren, the hills eroded, and the climate changed and became harsher. The Madrileños are proud of their fortitude and they are deeply hurt if you suggest that they do not live in the worst climate, short of Siberia, which any human being can suffer or support, be he never so hardy, but as a matter of plain fact the climate of the capital is a great deal maligned. I have spent several Augusts in Madrid and hardly ever found the heat unendurable; nor have I known a winter when, however savage the bite of the snow-laden winds, an entire week passed when one could not sit in the open air and dawdle over one's coffee in the sunshine.

Summer and winter you will, five or six days out of seven, see those deep, clear, blue skies which the Spaniards call 'Velázquez skies', either cloudless or else with a few high, white clouds racing across them like sailing clippers. The bright clear light which drenches a fine day in Madrid, especially in September and October, is rarely to be seen anywhere else. In the words of Señor González Ruano, Madrid is a city where light is more important than colour, grace more than beauty. No painter has been able to capture this peculiar luminosity. The nearest is Goya in *La Pradera de San Isidro* in the Prado. One or two of the French Impressionists might have succeeded, but none of them, as far as I know, ever came to paint in Madrid.

But when all is said and done it must be admitted that the climate of Madrid is treacherous and changeable, (oddly feminine, in fact, in such a very masculine country), for the city is built on a mountain-top which is over two thousand feet high even though it may be five or six hundred miles across. There is a local saying to the effect that the air of Madrid is so subtle that it can snuff out a man's life without snuffing out a candle. Therein, I have observed, it is matched by some of the locally produced razor blades, which are so subtle that they can lay your cheek open without cutting your bristles.

In the heat of summer, well-to-do Madrileños escape to the sea or the mountains, or at any rate pack their families off thither. A grass widower is called, for some odd reason, Rodríguez, and a man in the unhappy position (which is very apt to happen in the summer) of having both his wife and his mistress out of town at the same time will sadly say of himself: 'Soy Rodríguez y Rodríguez.' Some gatos own or hire chalets in the Guadarrama villages or in El Escorial and thence commute into the city in the summer. The poorer folk will be found sitting all night outside their houses or at the café tables which spread out over all the open spaces such as the Plaza de Santa Ana, waiting for the cool breeze which in Madrid always blows just before the dawn. (In summer the Plaza de Santa Ana, where tiny children play and race about until the small hours of the morning, provides the most agreeable open-air entertainment in Madrid. I have a friend who goes down to sit there and watch it three or four evenings a week.) Probably most of them have had a siesta, but the number of people in this very leisurely, sauntering city who tell you they never take a siesta is almost as surprising as the number who tell you they dislike bullfights or who shame your tardiness by turning up for an appointment to a split second. In Madrid they use up fewer units of energy per diem than in, say, Chicago and there is probably no one in the world who can do with less sleep than the born Madrileño.

The Plaza Mayor

Whatever its limitations the 'Austrian' style of architecture did at least produce one of the loveliest squares in the world in the Plaza Mayor, remarkable alike for its perfect symmetry and for the curious oblique, oddly angled street openings which recall Palladio's fantastic Olympian Theatre in Vicenza. The Plaza Mayor, a hundred and twenty metres long by a hundred wide, was created by Juan Gómez de Mora for Philip III, who was jealous of Henri IV's new Place Royale in Paris, and it was inaugurated on May 15th, 1620, with an eight-day fiesta for the beatification of San Isidro, the patron saint of Madrid. The balconies of its sixty-eight five-storey houses are said to have held some fifty thousand people. Royalty and Infantas watched the sometimes rather gruesome shows from the Casa de la Panadería or Municipal Bakery, the frescoed and very Austrian building on the north or Calle Mayor side. For the great spectacles such as the removal of the head of the conspirator Don Rodrigo Caldéron in 1621 and the fivefold canonisation of the

ALVAREZ ORTEGA.

Plaza Mayor

SS. Isidore, Ignatius, Theresa, Francis Xavier and Philip Neri in the following year (celebrated with bull-fights, fireworks and a new Lope de Vega comedy) first-floor balconies retailed at twelve ducats, second-floor at eight, third-floor at six and fourth-floor at four. It was at a bullfight here that the notorious amorist, the Count of Villamediana, sometimes thought to be the original of Don Juan, waved and smiled at Philip IV's young queen. She turned to her husband, beside her on the balcony, saying: 'He pics well, doesn't he?' 'Yes', agreed the King drily, 'he pics well, but I think he pics a little bit too high.' Next day the body of the temerarious toreador was found in an alley, run through with a sword.

Prices were high also for the numerous *autos de fé* which were celebrated here and which lasted anything up to twelve hours. On one day in 1680 eighty crypto-Jews were tried, of whom twenty-one were burned. Here is the description from the records of one dangerous heretic: 'Blanca Nogueira, spinster, born in the Kingdom of Portugal, and resident in the Court; aged 15, tall, wide nose, large black eyes, pointed chin and white skin'; and another: 'José Alonso, who sold cords in the streets; short of stature, round-faced, brown hair and pock-marks.'

With true Spanish tact, there was no *auto de fé* when the heretic Prince of Wales, later to become Charles I of England, made his romantic dash to Madrid to woo the King of Spain's daughter. Instead, he was shown bull-fights, horse-races and, to his considerable astonishment, a procession of hundreds of monks with ashes and crowns of thorns on their heads, carrying skulls and beating their breasts with stones.

Heretics condemned at an *auto de fé* were taken away
to be burnt at the Puerta de la Cebada, but executions of
common criminals used to take place here until 1765.
For a garrotting a scaffold was erected in front of the
Bakehouse, the Panadería, while beheadings were appropriately enough performed opposite in front of the House
of the Butchers, the Casa de la Carnicería. It was, perhaps,
with an equal appreciation of the fitness of things that
royal weddings were usually inaugurated with bull-
fights.

The last bullfight in the Plaza Mayor celebrated the
unhappy marriage of Isabel II in 1847. The next year the
equestrian statue of the creator of the Plaza, Philip III,
with his stiff ruff and his duckbill nose, was set up in the
middle and there could be no more *corridas*.

A Not-So-Hair Shirt

Very few people in Madrid wear hats (I hazard the guess
that not many hats can survive much getting in and out of
Madrid taxis), but there is a fascinating men's hat-shop
near the north-east corner of the Plaza Mayor, which
contains every known variety of hat—bullfighters'
monteras, military helmets, berets, *charro* hats from
Salamanca, waterproof hats, top-hats, opera-hats, shovel
hats, jockey caps, straw caps, crash-helmets, beavers—
every known variety of hat except a bowler, which has
only once been seen in Madrid when it is said to have
attracted considerable astonishment on the head of a
distinguished English novelist.

In the neighbouring street, the Calle de Postas, which

runs from the Plaza towards the Puerta del Sol, are four curious shops (I believe the only ones in Madrid) which specialise in the miscalled penitent's shirts. They are worn for a certain length of time by people who have made a vow to some saint or image or effigy. They are usually connected with recovery from an illness or the much desired birth of a child. (I knew a Legionary in the Nationalist column which was racing to relieve Toledo in the autumn of 1936 at such a rate of knots that the fall of the city was clearly a matter of days. 'I was so worked up that I made a vow to Our Lady to remain chaste until Toledo was taken', he told me solemnly and was rather shocked at my irreverence when I grinned.) These shirts come in about fifty different colours, a different one for every popular saint. Presumably there is one for the field, although I never asked.

There is a catch to them, nevertheless. A well-known London journalist, when visiting Spain, found these shirts extremely original and, quite unaware of their significance, bought two or three. Over drinks at the bar of the British-American Club in Madrid he told the story of how, sitting outside a café in Seville, he was tapped on the shoulder by a friendly priest, who asked: 'And what vow have you taken, young man?'

Everyone agreed that the best way to avoid such embarrassing incidents was not to wear these undeniably elegant shirts in Spain but to keep them until he got back to London, where, of course, nobody would know what they were. Bill Lewis, who had been in on the discussion at the Club, afterwards told me delightedly how, the next time he found himself in London, he had dropped into the York Minster in Dean Street and seen his bohemian friend sitting at the bar wearing the lovely purple shirt, tied with a golden cord and tassels at the neck, which dedicated him to *El Jesús de Gran Poder*. Coming up from behind, he tapped him on the shoulder and said: 'And what vow have you taken, young man?'

CHAPTER THREE

Eating in Old Madrid

There are three or four well-known restaurants round the Plaza Mayor. At the south-west corner of the great Plaza is a flight of stone steps under an Arch called the Arco de los Cuchilleros—the Arch of the Cutlers. At the top is El Púlpito, which specialises in roast sucking-pig and chicken cooked in sherry. At the bottom of the steep steps (down which a Spanish friend of mine once rolled all the way into the middle of the street) is the yet more famous Cuevas de Luis Candelas. Luis Candelas was a popular bandit of a century and more ago. (Brigands tend to be popular figures in Spain.) It belongs to a retired bull-fighter called Felix Colomo. On the wall is the head of a brown bull with the satirical couplet below:

> *Mató este toro Colomo*
> *Pero no sabemos como!*

Even if you do not intend to eat there you can go in and look at the Caves of Luis Candelas for ninety centimos, the price of a glass of wine, for they are built upon the pattern of all the typical Madrid *tascas*, a bar in front and the dining room behind. To reach some of the best restaurants in Madrid such as Valentín in the Calle de San Alberto and the Baviera in the Calle de Alcalá you

have to go through a squalid bar, ankle-deep in dirty
paper napkins and the exoderms of shellfish, with grubby
men drinking red wine by the glass and probably a rather
woebegone whore sitting gloomily in the corner—
doubtless what the rather individual English translations
of Spanish menus like to describe as the 'tart of the
house'.

Opposite the Caves of Luis Candelas is a little seventeenth-century *tasca* called the Hangman's Inn, El Mesón
del Verdugo, where I coveted a Talavera tile set in
the wall with the prudent and almost unanswerable
advice: 'If you drink to forget, please pay before
drinking.'

Further down the Street of the Cutlers is the two-
hundred-year-old Restaurant Botín, to which Mr.
Hemingway's hero, Robert Jordan, repaired to eat the
famous roast sucking-pig, little creatures no larger than
hares and so tender that the proprietor can carve them not
with a knife but with the side of a plate.

On the other side of the Calle Mayor, in the Plaza del
Comandante Las Morenas, is El Hogar Gallego, a
Galician restaurant popular all the year round for its
sea-food and in the summer also for its cool garden,
where one eats under the trees. Señor Evaristo Varela,
the owner, has his own oyster-beds at Santa Cristina near
La Coruña and imports all his fish and molluscs and his
white Ribeiro wine direct from Galicia.

Restaurants in General

If there is one thing more flattering to one's self-esteem
than the welcome you get from the waiter when you go
into a Madrid restaurant, it is the enthusiastic '*Muy bien!*'
with which he applauds your impeccable taste in food.
Even if you have not brought off a beautiful and perilous
faena in the bullring or kicked the winning goal against
Barcelona in the Bernabéu Stadium, you have unerringly,
he makes you feel, picked the three winners from the list
of runners which he has brought you. You call the waiter
(if you happen to share the ordinary English inhibitions
about hissing at people) with an '*Oigá!*' which means
'Listen!'—a favourite imperative in a land where nobody
ever does. If, as I believe, the story is apocryphal about the
visitor who for weeks thought '*No funciona*' was the
Spanish for a lift, the one is certainly true of the foreigner
who long thought *oigá* was the Spanish for a waiter. The
bill has changed its sex in the crossing of the Tyrrhenian
Sea, for the Italian *il conto* becomes *la cuenta* in Spain.

Many Madrid restaurants, such as the Baviera, serve
large portions. It is not possible as a rule to order half a
portion if you are by yourself, but if you can agree with
your companion on the same dishes you can order one
portion between the two of you—*una ración para los dos*.
That way you can have a four-course meal without either
overeating or overspending. Service is on the bill but you
should leave about five pesetas as an acknowledgement to
the waiter of his existence and individuality. That is for
one or two people; naturally, it will be more for a larger
party.

Meals Mañana

It is safest to assume that everything is likely to be at least an hour and a half later than in England. Thus, if you are accustomed to have your first drink of the evening at half past six in England, you would be wise to put it off until eight o'clock in Madrid if you do not want to find yourself with a skinful by the time dinner comes along.

Madrid does not rise early. In its own phrase it is *poco madrugador*. Few people are about before nine and the shops open at their leisure any time after that. The morning papers are seldom on sale much before half past eight, and as late as ten o'clock I have been told by my paper-seller in the centre of the city that *ABC* was not yet out.

Office hours in winter run from nine or ten until one, half past one or two, and from four thirty to eight or eight-thirty; in summer from nine till twelve and from four till eight—or, quite simply, from eight until two. From the beginning of June and for the rest of the summer, the banks close at midday instead of at half past one as in winter—a fact which is worth remembering. Saturday is a working day except for Government departments. Shops close on Sundays and fiestas except for bars and cakeshops, although bakers keep open in the morning.

The smart cocktail bars open at midday. I have found the Palace Bar and the Balmoral almost empty at one o'clock in the afternoon and at half past seven in the evening, when they would be most crowded in any other capital, but crammed at three and at ten with pre-prandial sippers. Except in the big hotels where foreigners go, luncheon begins at about two and people drift in until about half past three. In the more crowded restaurants it is hard to find a free table at half past three. (I have stayed in a country inn in Andalusia where the dining room only opened at half past three in the afternoon and half past ten at night.) In the average restaurant the kitchen closes at four in the afternoon and at midnight, but some of the smaller *tascas*, such as the Alboroque in the Calle del Caballero de Gracia, where the kitchen is more of a family matter, keep open much later.

Until a period of what by Spanish standards can be termed austerity was ushered in by the Civil War, the hours seem to have grown progressively later (possibly, as Mr. H. V. Morton suggests, because of the introduction of street lighting). A century ago, the two main meals, as in England, were between eleven and twelve (the word *merienda* meaning luncheon is said to be derived from the Latin *meridies* or midday) and at about five in the afternoon. As late as 1865 Pérez Galdós wrote that the life of the capital finished at midnight, but sixty years later Ramón Gómez de la Serna found it in full swing at three or four in the morning. Today, the reaction is towards midnight or one o'clock closing except for a few theatrical cafés such as the Gijón. The bars generally close at half past two and the nightclubs much later.

The late General Primo de Rivera attempted to europeanise Spanish eating hours but, like Philip V who clamped down on bullfighting, and Charles III, who tried to abolish the cloak (comparing the Spaniards, like a typical benevolent autocrat, to 'naughty children who quarrel with their good nurse when she wants to wash them'), he found that there are certain *cosas de España* beyond even the power of an absolute ruler to change.

When the Bellman lectured on the habits of the Snark:

> *Its habit of getting up late, you'll agree,*
> *That it carries too far, when I say*
> *That it frequently breakfasts at five o'clock tea*
> *And dines on the following day,*

he was not addressing a Madrileño crew, for that would have appeared to them a perfectly normal timetable.

If you go out to dinner in a Madrid house, you are invited for ten o'clock, sit or stand around sipping drinks for an hour and eventually sit down to table at about eleven. I have before now sat down to dinner at half past two in the morning. All of which goes to show how difficult a town Madrid is to get to bed in—and, naturally, to get up in.

Actors, in particular, have a hard life in comparison with their English colleagues, for they have two performances every evening. The matinée starts at seven o'clock and the evening performance at eleven. With two shows daily and a comparatively small public to cater for, runs are short and the actors spend most of the day rehearsing for the next play. In the last century the Apolo Theatre in the Calle de Alcalá, where the Banco de Vizcaya now stands, put on four shows a night, with the last one beginning at two in the morning. Work in the film studios, on the other hand, generally starts at the civilised hour of 2 p.m.

There is a great deal to be said in favour of the late

luncheon hour, for it means that, with no need to get up early, you can have a good long morning of work or sightseeing, dawdle over your aperitive, lunch at two or three, take a siesta and devote the evening to the streets and cafés, always remembering that Richard Ford, adapting Pope, said that 'Spanish man is—next to Spanish woman—the proper study of mankind'.

The Kitchen of Madrid

The Province of Madrid itself produces little to eat except the vegetables from the market gardens in the Jarama and Tagus valleys, strawberries and asparagus from Aranjuez during the season, and the occasional trout from the Guadarrama. All the same, the finest food from all over Spain flows daily into Madrid, where the immigrants have brought with them their local fare and tastes and opened regional restaurants. Fish and molluscs of all sorts from Galicia (for the coast between Vigo and El Ferrol is perhaps the richest in the world for shellfish); elvers from the Basque rivers; prawns from Valencia; all these, known only to a handful of travellers and gastronomes until the coming of refrigeration, are now on the counter of every *tasca* in Madrid.

Madrid has become little less than a paradise for ichthyophagoi in spite of its distance from the sea, for every night refrigerator-trains and refrigerator-lorries bring supplies of fresh seafood from the teeming, fecund Atlantic coasts. You can watch them in the morning arriving and unloading at the wholesale fish market near the Puerta de Toledo.

Meat

As in Italy the meat is generally veal and is generally tough, for in this warm climate it has always been the custom to serve it almost immediately after killing and, even now that the butchers have refrigerators, they seldom bother to unfreeze it sufficiently. The best meat, probably, is a Castilian regional dish called *cochinillo asado*, the tender roast sucking-pig, so young that it has crackling but very little fat on it, which can be sampled at its best at Botín's and Julián Rojo's; or *corderito*, roast sucking-lamb, which is a speciality of Valentín's. Chicken is cooked in a variety of ways, as is partridge, which in Spain replaces the ubiquitous quail and pigeon of Italy. Especially good is *perdiz estofada*, partridge stewed in white wine.

On account of the toughness of the meat, the staple dish of Madrileños in the old days was *cocido madrileño*, also known by the names of *coci*, *peri*, *puchero* and, in Andalusia, *olla*. Many restaurants still make it a *plat du jour* one day a week, generally Monday. It is a stew of dry beef, chicken, bacon, smoked ham, Cantinpalos sausage, potatoes, beans, turnips, carrots, cabbage, blood sausage, marrowbone, pork, ham and the chickpeas or *garbanzos* locally known in Madrid as 'gabriels'. Every true *gato* avers that it has to be cooked in Lozoya water, just as every Dubliner denies that stout can be made without Liffey water.

The traditional technique for tackling this rather daunting dish is to make the famous *tres vuelcos* of it. First you tip up the *puchero* (which means an earthenware dish) and drink the stock soup, mopping it up with bread; secondly, empty out the *puchero* into the soup plate and return to it the meat, sausages and so forth while you eat the vegetables; lastly, if you are still alive, eat the meat. Nowadays a *cocido* is expensive, but in the old days, when it was the daily fare of Madrileños, the impecunious bohemian or student could buy a solid three-course meal for eighty centimos. After a luncheon of *cocido* he probably supped on a *guisado de Madrid*, a stew of game, rabbit, chicken, bacon, herbs, garlic, onions, peppers and wine.

Of the same *pot au feu* type as these two are the *pote* from Galicia and the *fabada asturiana* from Asturias. They are based on white beans, young cabbage, potatoes, pork and lard. The simple and practical recipe for most of these dishes is, in fact, to throw everything you have into a pot and cook it.

Another characteristic local dish is *callos a la madrileña*, which consists of squares of tripe, cooked in oil with fine veal, blood sausage, bits of ham and spices, and served with the traditional piquant red sauce of Madrid, which is made of wine, tomatoes, garlic, oil, saffron and red peppers. (For myself, I consider the sauce to be the only redeeming feature of the dish.) Snails or *caracoles a la madrileña* are done with the same sauce, or they may be cooked with oil, flour, bacon, garlic, cummin and pepper. Down in the Barrios Bajos you may occasionally be made a little queasy by the smell of frying candle-grease. It will be *gallinejas*, which are tripe fried in tallow.

Traditionally a meal starts off with soup, hors d'œuvres or shellfish. In the summer, everyone should try an Andalusian soup called *gazpacho*. Served ice-cold in a bowl, it is made of tomato, onion, cucumber and pepper ground up in oil and vinegar, and may be embellished by the customer with a number of little sippets such as cubes of toast, tomato, peppers and cucumber. It is said to be of Moorish origin—like so many much worse and better things in Spain.

The traditional *entremeses* or hors d'œuvres consist of hard-boiled eggs, salad, tomato, onion, cucumber, tunny, sardines, anchovies, black olives, pepper, ham and Lord knows what else. Note that *jamón* by itself means *jamón de Serrano* or raw smoked ham. Our cooked ham is called *jamón york*. Roll the 'r' in York for they will not understand 'Yo'k'.

Codology

The variety of seafood is enchanting but also bewildering, and the Madrileños eat it not only at meals but as a snack in bars, *marisquerías, cervercerías* and cafés. Sample the variety at the Monterrey in the Gran Vía, the Café Tropical in the Alcalá, or the Macarena in the Calle de Nuñez de Arce, if you want to see what shellfish can be when they try, feetless though they are, to rise to their full glory. 'Poverty and oysters always seems to go together', observed Sam Weller, and though shellfish are not by any means cheap the Madrileños, who are always supposed to be so hard-up, eat an enormous quantity of them without seeming to go broke. Indeed, in a town where dinner is served from ten o'clock onwards, many impatient citizens stanch their appetite with shellfish and beer in the evening.

I have amused myself by making a list, doubtless very

incomplete, of the infinite variety which you can find on the counters of these bars. Oysters (in the Ostrería or Casa de las Ostras in the Calle de la Cruz, half a dozen oysters cost about half a crown including a glass of sherry or champagne); *almejas*—clams; *mejillones*—mussels; *quisquillas*—shrimps; *gambas*—prawns; *langostinos*—larger prawns; *carabineros*—big red prawns; *cigalas*—hard-shelled Dublin Bay prawns or scampi; *langostas*—craw-fish; *bogabantes*—English-type lobsters; *bueyes del mar* or 'sea-oxen'—Cornish-type crabs; *centollas*—large, cold, raw spider-crabs; *changurros*—smaller, prepared, hot spider-crabs (the *granzevole* of the Upper Adriatic); *nécoras*—small crabs; *cangrejos*—little red freshwater crayfish (the technique, as with *cigalas*, is to take the point of a knife and cut the underside of the tail down one side, when the hard carapace will peel off easily without hurting your fingers); *boquerones* or whitebait; *changuetes de Málaga*—minute baby whitebait; *percebes*—goose barnacles, which are very good once you get over their resemblance to the paws of a dead monkey, black with green fingernails. The technique is to put your own thumbnail under that of the putrefying monkey and then pull with a slight twisting movement. Be careful a jet of salt water does not shoot out, as it can stain your clothes.

In addition to the expensive, usually German, imported caviares there are a number of different kinds of fish-roe on sale. Particularly good are the *huevos de atún* or tunny-roe, which is to be bought at Rivas y Alba in the Calle de los Peligros, and the Norwegian herring-roe paste, which is served on bread as a snack at a little oyster bar called the Viña de Oro in the Plaza de Santa Barbara.

To see fish at its most attractive go to any of the retail

markets. Madrid housewives buy their food partly in shops but even more in the street markets, of which there are many. The one in the Corredera Alta is very characteristic and is said to be the cheapest in Madrid. The most central, perhaps, is the Carmen between the Calle de Carmen and the Calle de Montera. Notice with what loving care the different-coloured and different-shaped fishes are arranged in patterns and circles like the artful creations of an expert chef or pastry-cook. Almost one feels that these fish-artists could match the flower-artists who make the hardly less ephemeral carpets of flowers at Orotava and Genzano.

The best (if most expensive) seafood restaurant is the Korynto, the only place where I have found English-style crabs and lobsters and avocado pears (which are called *agapates*). The word *Cantábrico* or *Gallego* in the title or description of a restaurant means that you can be reasonably sure of good fish and shellfish. Much the same with a *Restaurant Vasca*, although in a narrower sense. The Basques, traditional fishermen of the Great Newfoundland Banks, specialise in *bacalao*, which is dried and salted cod. There are many ways of cooking *bacalao* (before the age of refrigeration almost the only fish heard of in Madrid except trout). The commonest are *bacalao al pilpil* and *bacalao al ajo* (both with garlic) and *bacalao alla vizcaina*; after the board-hard dried fish has been soaked for twenty-four hours, it is cooked in oil and served with tomatoes and sauce, when it really becomes very palatable. *Bacalao* can be sampled at its best in such restaurants as the Guri Toli (which is Basque for 'Our Place') in the square just behind the B.E.A. Terminal, the Guria ('Ours') in the Calle de Huertas, the Or Kompon in the

Calle de Miguel Moya or the Jai Alai just behind the
Post Office.

Another Basque speciality is *angulas a la bilbaina* or *a la
Aguinaga*, which are in season from October to April.
These baby eels look like bleached grass shoots or tiny
worms, with reproachful little eyes like black pinheads,
and are caught in large quantities where the fresh water of
the swift Cantabrian rivers turns to salt. They are boiled
in oil with garlic and red pepper in an earthenware dish
and served up in it sizzling hot with the oil still on the boil.
They must be eaten with a wooden spoon, for they take
the taste of metal, and they have the further peculiarity
that, unlike all other fish, they cannot be left to die but
have to be killed immediately. This is done by putting
them into a bucket of water diluted with nicotine.

Spaniards are fond of all sorts of cuttlefish under such
names as *calamares*, *chipirones*, *pulpos* and *púlpitos*. *Calamares en su tinta* are squids cooked in their own ink and
are better than they sound. Tough rubbery bits of squid
(rather like the cricket-bat handles one used drearily to
chew at school) generally play only too large a part in
the *zarzuela de pescado*, a Catalan *fritto misto* composed of
half a dozen kinds of dried fish, all tasting, if of anything
at all, the same.

Cocochas or cod's cheeks are another kind of fish not
generally found in England; they are usually done *pilpil*
fashion. Merluza or hake is a very common fish and is
to be recommended with green sauce—*en salsa verde*.
Other good fish are *lubina*, *rodoballo*, *mero* and *rape*. The
freshest fish in Madrid is reputed to be found in María
Aroca's fish restaurant at the bottom of the Calle de
Toledo almost opposite the wholesale fish market.

A *paella valenciana* consists of rice boiled yellow-brown with saffron and peppered like a current cake with prawns, shrimps, clams, polyps, pork, rabbit, pimientos, bits of chicken and so forth, served in an iron dish. It is very filling at the time but apt to leave you hungry later. There are a lot of mediocre *paellas* served in Madrid, and it is safest to order it in a Valencian restaurant such as La Barraca in the Calle de la Reina just off the Gran Vía or the Valencia in the Plaza de Callao.

The Trimmings

There is a great variety of Spanish delicatessen: salami which is oddly called *Imperial* (Salaam to Charles V?); *mortadela*, which speaks for itself; *morcilla*, which is a black blood sausage; *longaniza*, a red sausage; the piquant red *sobresada* from Majorca; *butifarra* from Catalonia; and popular local sausages from Vich, Pamplona and Salamanca. (Vich is as famous for its smoked ham as for the frescoes of José María Sert.) Another delicacy, to be found especially in the Barrios Bajos, is the testicles of bulls, called *criadillas*, which bullfighters like to eat, as savages eat the flesh of lions, to make them brave. A menu in the Bar Jeréz once translated this delicacy into English as 'battered bulls' balls'.

Spanish cheeses are few and insipid when compared with those of England and France. There is *manchego* from La Mancha, or when preserved in oil (and I think improved thereby) *manchego en aceite*; *bola*, an imitation Dutch cheese; *kramt*, an imitation Roquefort; *burgalese* and *Reinosa*, good straight cream cheeses from the North, and various processed gruyères from Santander. The only really strong cheese is the Cabrales from Asturias. I have never come across it in a restaurant but the cheese-fancier can sample it at the Casa Mingo, an Asturian place near the bottom of the Calle de Echegaray, where the waiter also pours draught cider in the traditional Asturian fashion, holding the glass at arm's length near his thigh and the jug above his head with the other hand. It is hit or miss but generally hit.

In winter the only fruit consists of oranges, bananas, apples and bullet-hard pears. Strawberries come in in March and, like asparagus, are grown on a large scale at Aranjuez. ('Strawberries' or *fresas* are wild strawberries; garden strawberries are 'big strawberries' or *fresones*.) Then come loquats or *nisperas*, cherries, apricots, peaches, plums, figs, melons, the little flat peaches called *para-guayas*, grapes and all the rest of the South European fruits. Last of all for a short season in December arrive the exotic *chirimoyas* or custard apples.

Dialling Tum

After all this gastronomic intelligence it is nice to know that Madrid restaurants, bars and cafés have the admirable custom of throwing in a free service of bicarbonate of soda upon request, not to mention talcum powder for taking out grease stains. Diarrhoea is a common com-plaint of many visitors from northern countries whose systems are not attuned to oil cooking (and Spain, which produces the finest olive oil in the world, has to export her crop to America for dollars and herself use a mixture which is 20% olive and 80% soya bean oil). The restaurant at Barajas airport is reputed to be one of the few places in Madrid where they cook in proper olive oil. If a crisis blows up just before going on an expedition to a bull-fight or to a theatre, take Tanagel capsules, which are very strong and quick-acting. For gentler action try Enterovioforma or Lacteol.

CHAPTER FOUR

The Sun Gate

The Calle Mayor runs into the Puerta del Sol, for centuries the centre of Madrid, of Spain and of a great part of the known world. From it all the streets radiated to the fifteen gates of the capital, and the roads to all corners of the Peninsula. Set in the pavement just outside the Gobernación, the large neo-classical building on the south side, is 'the navel of Spain', the stone on which is carved the distance in kilometres to the provincial capitals and from which all distances are reckoned. On the wall of the building another inscription declares the altitude, exactly 650·7 metres above sea-level—Mediterranean, be it noted, and not Atlantic, for it is reckoned from the door-sill of the Ayuntamiento at Alicante.

The building, still called the Gobernación, was formerly the Post Office from which all the postal, courier and diligence services of Spain started out; then it became the Ministry of the Interior and ever since the Civil War it has been the Headquarters of the Police or Seguridad, which rivals the Dirección General de Turismo as one of the most efficient organisations in the country.

The Puerta del Sol

Police

The police with whom foreigners have to deal in the
matter of visas, permits and what not, are the *Guardia de
Seguridad* or *Policia Armada*, who wear a grey uniform
with red bands round their caps like British Military
Police. They patrol the streets, keep order, guard public
buildings and embassies, handle foreigners' documenta-
tion, and perform most of the usual functions of police-
men. The famous Civil Guard, a para-military corps of
rural gendarmerie, may be seen at work if you go out
of Madrid—always in pairs, one on either side of the road.
The occasional ones to be seen in Madrid are probably
either on leave, on duty at HQ or on a course of some
kind. The *Carabineros* are Customs Police who guard the
frontiers without any very noticeable success against
smugglers, although there are some on duty in Madrid
at the airport and the stations. The fourth kind of police
are the *Guardias Urbanos*, the traffic police, who wear blue
in winter and white in summer, but white sun-helmets
whatever the weather.

It may be as well to mention that, while Spain is a good
country for the man who likes his liquor (for liquor is
cheap and on the whole not too bad), it is an exceedingly
bad one for the man who does not know how to hold it.
Gamberrismo or hooliganism is heavily stamped on and
the police, as is only natural in a country which has
recently emerged from a Civil War, tend to swing their
clubs first and ask questions afterwards when law and
order seem in danger of being disturbed. If no such
question arises, then a pleasant word in however bad

Spanish and a rather bewildered smile will go much further than bluster and argument.

Basic Spanish

When I was a war correspondent in Spain in 1937 I knew a lieutenant in the Irish Brigade who had spent a contented year on a minimal vocabulary consisting of *vino*, *coñac* and *casa de putas*. He was, of course, a man of few wants and simple tastes, and the average traveller (with no military organization at his back to feed him, clothe him, lodge him, move him and blow his nose for him) will probably find his needs more diverse and complicated than those of my Irish friend.

He would be very wise to try and acquire at least a smattering of Spanish—not a very difficult thing to do for anyone who has learned Latin and French at school. He will find that the Spaniards still talk a fairly pure and basic, even if considerably bent, Latin, and it is pleasant to hear semi-literate peasants eschewing our northern monosyllables and talking naturally in the fine sonorous Latinisms of Sir Thomas Browne. And what a drumming and atomic sense of doom is there in the sale notice I saw in the window of a department shop in the Gran Vía in Madrid—'*Liquidación Total a Qualquier Precio de Toda Existencia*'.

El idioma castellano still has a number of fascinating idiosyncrasies, for no two languages exactly correspond any more than two alphabets. What would a psychologist deduce, for example, from the fact that the Spaniards have only one word, *gastar*, for to spend and to waste?

They have only one word, *mañana*, for tomorrow and for morning, so that tomorrow morning is *mañana por la mañana* and tomorrow evening, paradoxically, *mañana por la tarde*. That brings us straight to the most awkward omission of all, the lack of any word for evening, the very time when the average Madrileño comes to life. One cannot say directly in Spanish: 'I shall be out all the afternoon but I shall be at home in the evening', for *la tarde* is the period from midday to dusk and *la noche* any time after dark. I use the adjective awkward from personal experience, for it is indeed little less than awkward when one sits down to write a note to send with a bunch of flowers to one's hostess on the morrow of a dinner-party. It seems ridiculous to thank her for a delightful afternoon which did not begin until ten o'clock; on the other hand if you write 'night' you may have her husband chasing you with a revolver. *Velada* is a possible word but very pedantic and not much used.

To compensate for these deficiencies, Spanish has one or two very useful verbs which we lack: e.g. *caber*, meaning to be able to be contained in; for example a quart *no cabe* a pint-pot. Another is *cobrar*, to be paid. '*Querría Usted cobrar?*'—'Would you like to be paid?'—you ask when you want to pay for your drink. For myself I find it rather fascinating that a gentleman should take his title from his means of locomotion and still, in the twentieth century, be a *caballero*, literally a horseman or cavalier. If the language were now in the process of formation would the word for a gentleman be *motorista*? No prizes for the answer.

The word *hidalgo* meaning a member of the lesser nobility, a slight cut above a *caballero*, is no longer heard in Spain, although it survives in print, in the names of a few clubs and societies. The irregular plural *hijosdalgo* reveals the origin of the word; the female of the species are even more irregular than their mates (much as they would hate to hear it said about them), for they are not *hijasdalgo* but *damas hijosdalgo*.

If you know only a few words of a foreign language, it is always fun to have a few good ones to show off with. Here are a few to try for size. *Tócame-Roque*, flimsy, phony, shaky, or on a weak wicket; *pordiosero*, a beggar; *madrugador*, an early riser; *trasnochador*, a nightbird; *andarín*, fond of walking; *tasquear*, to pubcrawl from one *tasca* to another; *faldero*, a man fond of a skirt (*falda*) and his feminine counterpart, a *pantalonera*; *muchedumbre*, a crowd; *guapa*, pretty, attractive (of a girl); *constipado*, having a cold. 'How is your husband?', I once asked a woman in Madrid. '*Pobrecito! Está constipadillo*,' she answered, with that Spanish love of diminutives.

The dry air and the central heating of Madrid combine to crack and dry the lips and, if you want to buy white lip-salve, you ask, rather surprisingly, for lip-cocoa, *cacao para los labios*—or, better still, send out the page-boy to buy it. In Spanish a page-boy is a *botones* or Buttons, as in *Aladdin*, and one finds oneself wondering whether he will ever be brought up to date (*reformado* is the Spanish word) and just called *zip*; probably not, for the Spanish for a zip-fastener is *cremallera*, and one could hardly have a page-boy who sounded like a cream-jug. '*Hombre!*', literally 'man' or, as we might say, 'manalive!' is a useful word for all occasions; it may be addressed to a customer by a waiter, to a woman by her husband, to a child by

its mother. I have even heard dogs and cats thus apostro-
phised.

The Cafés

When San Felipe el Real was pulled down, the functions
of the Lie Exchange were automatically taken over by
the cafés. In the last century, by my reckoning, there must
have been a couple of dozen in the Puerta del Sol and the
two or three fashionable streets which formed an eastward extension of it. Now only two or three are left
where formerly they were side by side, as they still are
in many provincial towns. Many owed such exotic names
as Londres, Lisboa and Paris, Universal, Levante, Oriental
and Colonial to the cosmopolitan influence exuded by the
kilometre stone and the posting terminus.

In the old days Madrid was (with the possible exception
of Vienna) the most famous city in Europe for cafés.
Yet only last year an English friend asked me: 'Why are
there so few cafés in Madrid?' The answer is that many
have perished in their long battle with the banks, and the
survivors have fallen victims to the jackal cafeterias and
milk bars. Though the few that are left are invariably
crowded, it must be hard to make them pay, for the
waiter will let you take up a table for hours after you have
finished a single cheap drink and never hang around or
ask what else he can bring you. Small profits and slow
returns! Writers, journalists and students work in cafés
and save their light and heating. A number of business
men maintain no offices but meet their friends and clients
in their regular café; their office rent amounts to a cup

of coffee every morning and another every afternoon.

Many *gatos* use their favourite café as a sort of extension or projection of their home, their drawing room or their study, for it is probably a good deal warmer, quieter and more comfortable than their crowded flats. In the average middle-class home, heated in winter only by braziers filled with charcoal or crushed olive stones, most of the rooms have been converted into bedrooms for the annual increment of children, and every stiff-backed chair in the *salón* is occupied by a maiden aunt or grandmother who has nowhere else to go except to church. The yelling infants have to be put to bed, the dinner has to be cooked, and the master of the house is turned out and told not to come back before ten.

The Madrileños may meet their friends and embrace them with the famous *abrazo*, each with the left arm round the other's shoulder, in a café or a bar every day for twenty years and never once enter each other's houses or meet each other's wives, for it is seldom that anybody except a member of the family is invited into a middle-class Spanish home. Polite remarks such as *Mi casa es suya* and *Aquí tienes tu casa* are no more intended to be taken literally than the *Que aproveche, señor!* or *Quiere comer?* with which a Spaniard will invite you to share his meal in a railway carriage. A sort of sexual *apartheid* prevails. The house is the domain of the woman; the street and the café that of the man. A Spaniard's home is his wife's castle.

Many men break their fast in a café on their way to work. In the last century the traditional breakfast was a tumbler of white coffee with four lumps of sugar, accompanied by half a roll of toasted French bread, which was known as a *media*. It cost forty centimos before the loss of the colonies in 1898 and seventy-five centimos afterwards. Indeed, for many poor students who could not afford even *cocido*, this was also their luncheon and dinner, varied by a cup of chocolate with the Majorcan bun called an *ensaimada*. Nowadays, the *media* has gone out and breakfast generally consists of *churros*, which are corrugated strips of batter cooked in boiling oil and sprinkled with sugar, croissants, brioches, *ensaimadas* or *buñuelos*, which are doughnuts and are also called *berlinesas*. A white coffee in Spanish is a *café con leche*, a black coffee a *café solo* and a coffee with a dash of milk a *café cortado*.

A tip of a peseta, or the odd centimos from the change, is enough for a single drink; or up to five for a party. There is no need to reckon up percentages, as service is already on the bill.

The pasteurised milk of Madrid is good, and like yoghourt can be bought by the glass in any *lechería*—which is not the kind of place it sounds like. A *leche merengada*, by the way, is not a kind of milk but an ice. A *granizada* is a drink of powdered ice with lemon or coffee poured over it, and a *blanco y negro* is a vanilla ice with black coffee.

To be had in a few cafés in the summer is a milky and refreshing drink which is not to be found anywhere outside Spain and is called *horchata*. It is made from the white juice of the *chufa* or tiger-nut, a striped ground-nut which grows, it is said, nowhere in the world except in the region of Valencia. Efforts to introduce it elsewhere, notably near Verona and in parts of Africa, have all failed. A delicious *horchata* was prepared for the King of Saudi

Arabia when he was an official guest in the Moncloa Palace. A large jug of this non-alcoholic beverage was made in the kitchen, and the king asked for a second; but it is to be feared that, for all his millions, he will have to wait for a third until he returns to Spain.

The best and the least unadulterated *horchata* is still to be found in Valencia, where twenty-five thousand quintals are grown on two hundred and fifty hectares of land and produce fifteen thousand litres of *horchata*, all of it drunk in Spain. *Horchata* is expensive and has to be made in quantity, so that the temptation is great to water it. It is only to be found in outdoor cafés and kiosks such as the ones in the Plaza de Cibeles and in certain café-bars which advertise it by cards in the windows. Owing to its price, the decline in quality and the competition of beer, Coca-Cola, *gaseosas* and the new fruit juices, the consumption in Madrid has been going down year by year.

If you go regularly to the same café you will notice certain of the tables filling up with the same people at the same time of the day, for many of the clients belong to a *tertulia*. The word (said, rather improbably, I would say, to be derived from the habit of the learned members of discussing Tertullian) is untranslatable into English, although it has something in common with both the German *Stammtisch* and the Italian *Conversazione*. It is a table or a corner of the bar where the same group meets to talk every day, twice a day, once a week, or whatever it may be—especially members of the same professional group—writers, painters, politicians, bullfighters, lawyers or doctors. Leaders of their professions each hold, or used to hold, their own regular *tertulias*, surrounded by eager disciples and sycophants. There are writers and journalists who still have their afternoon *tertulia* in the Café León in the Alcalá.

Where are the Cafés of Yesteryear?

The old-style cafés were characterised by red plush sofas and massive brass spittoons. The plush seats were backed by vast gilt-framed mirrors in which the members of the *tertulia* could measure every gesture and perfect each expression, whether they were politicians orating, poets reciting, actors declaiming or professors lecturing. Everyone was arguing, discussing, criticising, gossipping, speechifying, all at once, with each man having to shout to make himself heard even by himself, for in Madrid 'there are no listeners—only tired talkers', as Jack Yeats once remarked of his own Dublin.

The last survivor of the old red plush cafés was turned into a cafeteria in May of 1959—the Varela, on the corner of the Calle de los Preciados and the Plaza de San Domingo. Every Friday evening there was a *tertulia* called 'Verses at Midnight', a poetry recital in which the public took part. The presiding genius of the Varela was Emilio Carrère, the last popular poet of Madrid, who died in 1947. Above the seat where he sat and wrote and talked every night until the small hours the poets of Madrid placed a plaque reading '*Homenaje de los poetas de España*', a refreshing and unexpected evidence of solidarity on the part of that *genus irritabile*.

> *Poets of the world, unite!*
> *You have only your brains to lose!*

Of the well-known bohemian cafés almost the last left is the Gijón in the Paseo de los Recoletos. Writers go there to work over a cup of coffee in the mornings, and in the evenings artists, writers, lawyers, doctors and so forth hold their regular *tertulias*. Stage people come on there about half past one in the morning after their last performance is over. It is especially crowded on a Saturday night. But some of the younger bohemians consider the Gijón is becoming rather a show place and prefer to go to the cellars of the Sesamo in the Calle de Principe.

Now in the Puerta del Sol, survive only the Antiguo Café Levante on the shady side, and on the sunny side the Flor. A few steps up the Alcalá is the Universal, which was known in its heyday as Los Espejos or The Mirrors. In the eighteen-sixties it was the favourite haunt of Pérez Galdós, for there he was sure of meeting his compatriots of the Canarian colony. The Flor has a quick-service passport-photo service attached—a thing which is useful to know when you are sent out of the Seguridad and told to come back with photographs. The Universal has a restaurant upstairs where you can get a meal up to three in the morning—which is yet another thing worth knowing.

Of the old landmarks hardly anything survives except Lhardy's in the Carrera de San Jerónimo, which is a pastrycook's, delicatessen shop and restaurant founded in 1839 by a Swiss called Emile Lhardy. During the vogue of the French-inspired Romanticism Lhardy's became the fashionable place to drop in for soup or pastries. It was the haunt of dandies, politicians, writers, actors and bull-fighters, a place known for lovers' assignations and challenges to affairs of honour, until towards the end of the nineteenth century the popularity of the Café Fornos tended to pull Society away from the Carrera de San Jerónimo to the Alcalá. Go in there on a chilly morning and taste the excellent chicken broth. Behind the polished black and mahogany woodwork are enormous silver urns and samovars with the legend '*Thé*' practically erased by over forty thousand days of polishing. Except for the weighing machine and the cash register everything has been kept exactly as it was in the old days. Upstairs are rooms which can be reserved for private parties and banquets. They also are furnished in untouched high nineteenth-century style. The corridor which connects them is adorned by what is possibly the longest hat-rack in the world—a hundred and eighteen pegs in a row.

Of the vanished cafés of the Puerta del Sol, the first was the stormy Café Lorenzini on the corner of the Calle de Espoz y Mina, later known in turn as Las Columnas, Londres and lastly Puerto Rico. It was a favourite stamping ground for patriotic and republican orators. Liberal societies such as *Los Amigos del la Libertad* and *Los Hombres de Buena Fé* had their headquarters there. Their opponents, *Los Amigos del Orden*, used to gather in La Fontana de Oro, almost next door on the corner of the Calle de Victoria. The Café de Madrid on the corner of the Alcalá and the Pasaje de Iris was another favourite place for discussing politics and war at the end of the century.

Most of these cafés were associated with the names of some great men who could be seen and heard there every day. Goya frequented the narrow, smoky Café Levante on the corner of the Puerta del Sol and the Alcalá, where the intellectuals and middle classes assembled to play chess. Rubén Darío, the great Nicaraguan poet, used El Colonial at the entrance to the Alcalá, just opposite the Café de Paris, where he lived. In the Café Platerias in the Calle Mayor García Lorca used to write his poems. The playwright Jacinto Benavente held his *tertulias* in the Café Lisboa at the entrance to the Calle Mayor. Dr. Ramón y Cajal, the Nobel Prize winner, presided over the doctors first in the Café del Prado in the Plaza de Santa Ana, and later in the Café Suizo. Valle-Inclán, Ortega y Gasset, and other writers and intellectuals used to hold forth in La Granja del Henar in the Alcalá. (Both the Granja and the Negresco next door, the haunt of actors, comedians and bullfighters in the twenties, have been killed and built on by the Banco Popular de España.) The politician Melquíades Alvarez pontificated in El Oriental on the corner of the Puerta del Sol and the Calle de los Preciados in his great days as a reformist orator. El Imperial, where the Hotel de Paris now stands, was so large that it boasted ten clocks, in a city where nobody thought about the hour, and was much frequented by all the students of Madrid. Frascuelo the bullfighter divided his time between El Imperial and the Taberna de Lázaro López next door to the Eslava Theatre, where Lagartero and many other fighters and breeders used to gather, and the statesman Sagasta used to take his meals.

The most famous *tertulia* of all was the one known as the Venerable Crypt which was presided over every Saturday evening for twenty years in the Café del Pombo at Calle de Carretas 4 by Ramón Gómez de la Serna. Solano's picture of Ramón surrounded by his *tertulia* now hangs in the Museum of Modern Art in the Paseo de los Recoletos. The Pombo was frequented by all the writers of 'the generation of '98' and was a place of pilgrimage for foreign visitors. It exists no more and, to add insult to injury, the same building now houses a cafeteria called Tio Sam, decorated with pictures of Uncle Sam.

The War between the Cafés and the Banks

When it was driven from the Puerta del Sol, bohemia found its last refuge in the Calle de Sevilla in three cafés, El Suizo, El Inglés and El Divan. The bewhiskered quid-nuncs who laid down the law on world affairs were replaced at first by comedians and by bullfighters in their *traje corto*, and lastly, as far as El Suizo was concerned, by the clerks in the towering Banco de Bilbao which was built on its corner-site with the Alcalá.

Nowhere did the war between the cafés and the banks rage more fiercely than in the Alcalá, where not only the Suizo but the Acuarium, fashionable in the decade before the Civil War, El Negresco and La Granja del Henar have been bought up and replaced by banks. The *tertulias* of the Café Fornos, now the Riesgo, were really the first eastward displacement of the *solerinos*, as the denizens of the Puerta del Sol were called, and, more than any other café, it replaced the Mentidero to become what Carrère called 'the eyes and the ears of Madrid'. It was open day and night and the literary *tertulias* run by Vital Aza used to go on until the dawn. After the fourth house at the

Apolo Theatre it was practically *de rigueur* to go on there or to the opposition republican café, the Cruz de Malta in the Calle del Caballero de Gracia.

The solitary recorded victory in the rearguard battle of the cafés against the banks was won by the Café de los Correos which then occupied the corner site of the Puerta del Sol and the Calle de Arenal (where the pious Philip II had once set up a de luxe brothel for the solace of his noble vassals). Next door to it was the Madrid branch of the Crédit Lyonnais, which wished to expand and to take over the café. It had the authorisation of the landlord and declined to give way to the objections of the café-owner. After one refusal too many the latter said: 'Now it is for *you* to move, my dear Sir, because I have bought the whole building and I am the one who am throwing *you* out.' The bank had to find new premises, and in the end it was the Café Madrid which was killed to supply them.

From being a street of cafés, the Alcalá is now a street of banks and insurance offices. The Riesgo is almost the only true café left on the north side of the street, although the Tropical, which is a *marisquería*, the Elipa, which is a *cervecería*, the Baviera, which is a restaurant, and the Dolár, which is a cafeteria, all put chairs out in the summer.

It is the milk bars and cafeterias which have now become the great rivals to the cafés. The former, called *granjas* or farms (which I take to be our word 'grange'), originally served mainly dairy products but they now sell snacks and alcoholic drinks, including very stiff cocktails, as well, and are hardly distinguishable from the cafeterias. Coffee machines flash and splutter and steam, and the old-style café waiter, with his short black coat, long white apron and a dozen spoons stuck in his sash, is replaced by a chorus line of uniformed young women in theatrical make-up. These places like to ape America and they bear such names as Béisbol (which is Spanish for baseball), Ike, California, Denver, Nebraska, Miami, Texas, Ohio, Niagara, Tulsa, Pennsylvania and, frankly, Dolár.

What with banks in the Alcalá and these cafeterias and milk-bars in the Gran Vía, there are few cafés left in their former stronghold.

CHAPTER FIVE

Fiestas

On the roof of the Gobernación is the clock which is in direct electric contact with the Observatory at Atocha and gives the official time. It is the Spanish Big Ben. Under the roof of the little clock tower is a golden ball which descends punctually on the stroke of noon and then ascends again. Provincials come to look at the sight and the *gatos* themselves set their watches by it. Once a year, or rather in the queer crevice between the years, illuminated with electric bulbs, it descends and reascends at midnight to usher in the New Year. It is *la Noche Vieja*.

Fireworks explode in all directions and as much of Madrid as can crowd into the Sol equips itself with paper hats and false noses and tries to make as much noise as possible with whistles, singing and dancing to drums improvised from frying pans and saucepan lids. There is an old tradition that the year will be lucky for anyone who eats twelve grapes between the twelve strokes of midnight. So the merrymakers go armed with a little paper bag or a basket of twelve grapes. (They are believed to be most efficacious if popped into one's mouth by a *señorita guapa*.) Then the racket is resumed and kept up until dawn.

A similar rowdy open-air party takes place six days later at Twelfth Night, which in Spain is called *Los Reyes*, the Kings. *Reyes*, not Christmas, is the traditional time to distribute presents to all the children in memory of the gifts brought by the three Kings to the Infant Jesus. In the cribs set up for Christmas, the Kings start far away and are moved every day a little closer until January the Sixth, when they reach out to make their offerings, and the children also receive their presents and eat the traditional delicacy of *Reyes*, a kind of sponge cake called *roscón*.

Every year at *Reyes* a calvacade of Magi starts at six in the evening from the Retiro and proceeds along the Alcalá to the Ayuntamiento. First comes the unavoidable brass band; then a flock of rather puzzled sheep; next, peasants in regional dress carrying torches, who presumably represent the shepherds; then a squadron of helmeted Roman cavalry; then the Three Kings, one of them, of course, the traditional negro, with their attendant *cuadrillas*, followed at the end by the populace of Madrid. Once arrived at their destination, the Magi present their gifts at the crib set up in the Ayuntamiento while the children hand in the Kings' letters specifying the presents they would like.

The other procession in January is that of San Antonio Abad—St. Antony Abbot, the white-bearded, black-robed hermit, shown in so many pictures being tempted by devils, who became the patron saint of animals from the fact of his being companioned in all his tribulations by a small black pig.

La Romería de San Antón takes place on January 17th and at half past three in the afternoon an assembly of diverse beasts is paraded outside the church of San Antón in the Calle de Hortaleza; they are first of all blessed and sprinkled, and then escorted by mounted police in full dress down the Calle de Barceló. There are men and girls in *traje del campo* mounted on caracoling horses; there are dressed-up dogs; there are beautifully groomed mules and asses in their gayest caparisons.

Originally the main beneficiaries of the blessings were the pigs and other domestic animals belonging to the local farmers, who used to ride in with their pretty dairy-maids on their bedecked, bebelled and betasselled mules and mingle with the grooms of the abbots and the gentry with theirs. Originating after deliverance from a plague in the sixteenth century, the fiesta used to be little less than a riot, with hucksters' stalls and a fairground. Now it is a very decayed affair since hooves have been replaced by wheels. Cars are blessed in the Paseo de Coches in the Retiro on St. Christopher's Day. The pig-farms are covered with mountains of bricks and mortar; there are not many dogs in Madrid anyhow; and fighting bulls are for obvious reasons not eligible for a blessing, quite apart from their inherent unsuitability for walking in processions through the city.

In the old days Carnival was the gayest time in Madrid, but there is nothing left of it except a few private dances in hotels and clubs, and painted children in fancy dress being dragged rather reluctantly round the streets. The wearing of masks has been abolished by the present régime not only for political and moral reasons but on account of the number of private knifings which it made so easy; so there is an end to the flirtations, masquerades and disguises, to such saturnalia as the Burial of the

Sardine, which Goya painted, and to the processions of floats and cars in the Castellana, Recoletos and Rosales. Still, a joke is a joke, and Carnival must have been sometimes a little much when you could not venture out of your house day or night without tripping over a cord stretched across the street, having your hat snatched or being pelted with stale fish or eggs filled with water.

The first Friday in March is a local Madrid fiesta when the pious queue to kiss the image of Jesús Nazareno at the Capuchin church in the Calle de Medinaceli just behind the Palace Hotel. (The image itself, perhaps the most fashionable in Madrid, was spirited away in 1936 at the outbreak of the troubles and recovered in Switzerland in 1939.) If you go to this church, notice the Tussaud-like tableau in the left aisle which vividly illustrates Spanish realism and goes far beyond the human hair, linen kilts and velvet robes of the images. In the carpenter's shop at Nazareth, with all the figures lifesize, and real hacksaws and carpenters' tools lying on the bench, Mary is spinning on a distaff, while Jesus holds a hammer in one hand and a bunch of nails in the other. In a tiny cage on the wall is a stuffed (one hopes) bird.

Here in Madrid one is always being surprised at the way in which this world and the next seem to mingle and interpenetrate each other like land and water on a map of Finland. Girls bear names like Concepción, Asunción, Peligros, Milagros, Soledad and even, in one case I knew, Reyes—Kings. A dairy just behind my hotel was called La Lechería de la Immaculada Concepción. Nobody apparently saw any blasphemy when Godoy arrogated to himself the title of the Prince of Peace. Similarly the churches have incongruous (at least to us) pieces of the lay world intermingled everywhere, such as the pair of kitchen scales on the tomb of Ferdinand VI in Santa Barbara. *Viva la Muerte!* was the battle cry of the Foreign Legion—Long Live Death!

Holy Week

Holy Week is, of course, the time to witness religious manifestations, but most Madrileños who can do so take the opportunity to get out into the country for a few days and they make little attempt to match their own processions against those of Seville, Murcia or Valladolid. There are, however, several very typical ones worth seeing.

On Palm Sunday, the palm branches are blessed in church and taken home to adorn the windows and balconies of the pious. According to Richard Ford, they are, or were, held to be extremely efficacious as protection against lightning. Many of them are cut, bent and plaited into such elaborate basketwork patterns that one would hardly believe they could be made from a single frond. They come from the great palm forest at Elche, where the trees are so intensively cultivated that many even have their individual names. (Visitors to Alicante may remember a palm tree opposite the Bar Club on the Esplanade called Professor Don Ipólito Rodríguez Pinilla.) It takes a month and a half to cut the five million branches which are sold every Easter in Spain. Only the male palms are used, as they do not in any case bear dates. They are bleached by being tied up and muffled in sacking for a few months before being cut.

At midday, a procession of children starts from the Convent of the Descalzas Reales, the Royal Shoeless, to commemorate the Entry into Jerusalem. Jesus rides on an ass and is followed by three thousand children bearing palms, who perambulate the Gran Vía and the other neighbouring streets. Details of the evening processions can be found in the morning papers.

Of the Holy Thursday ceremonies, the most interesting is the Sevillian procession of the Confraternity of Jesús de Gran Poder and of the Virgen de la Esperanza, generally known as La Macarena, which sallies forth at half past eight in the evening from San Isidro and can be seen as it goes through the Puerta Cerrada, the Calle Mayor, the Plaza de la Villa, the Plaza Mayor, the Puerta del Sol, the Plaza de la Provincia, the Calle de Atocha, the Plaza de Tirso de Molina and so back by the Calle de Toledo. For all the crowds it is not hard to find a place to see the procession since it lasts for no less than five hours on account of the numerous halts to sing *saetas*, the agonised laments or hymns to Christ and the Virgin sung in Andalusia in Holy Week. For this procession is not an old Madrid tradition at all. It is, in fact, neither old nor Madrid. The whole atmosphere is that of Seville. The Confraternity of the Macarena, largely composed of Sevillian residents, was founded in 1940 and the first procession took place in 1942. First come three hundred Nazarenes wearing masks and high dunce-like caps, with ropes round their waists. Then follow the images of Jesús de Gran Poder and La Macarena, which are exact copies of the originals venerated in Seville, on floats borne by thirty-two bearers in the case of Christ and thirty-eight in that of the Virgin, for her twenty-metre-long robe of black velvet is embroidered with forty kilograms of gold.

On Good Friday the churches are filled with the faithful. If you go to church, you will notice how the doors shriek and wail, as one can imagine Goya's witches doing if canvas could utter. I have had it explained to me that Spanish doors are so made that they cannot be oiled without first being taken off their hinges. In the churches, where the congregation is all the time drifting in and out, the doors keep up a shrill eldritch cacophony which can drown an organ, to say nothing of a mere sermon.

In the early hours of Good Friday the parish of Buen Suceso organises a Via Crucis of penitents down to the Parque del Oeste to plant crosses. At half past seven in the evening one of the greatest processions of Holy Week, that of the Confraternity of Jesus the Nazarene, issues from the Medinaceli church and passes through the Carrera de San Jerónimo, the Puerta del Sol, the Alcalá, the Plaza de Cibeles and so home at nine o'clock. The image is carried on an illuminated float and the great procession of Confraternity members is headed by mounted police and a drum and cornet band. Banners wave aloft and the Capuchins direct the hymns and prayers through loudspeakers. Enormous crowds collect to watch the procession.

At eleven the Procession of Silence, organised by the Brotherhood of Crusaders for the Faith, starts from the Puerta del Sol where, and in the neighbouring streets, some four hundred thousand sightseers assemble. Accompanied by their priests, over seven thousand Nazarenes belonging to the different Confraternities march in the Procession, many of them barefoot, carrying candles or great wooden crosses, and some of them trailing heavy chains. The members of each Confraternity carry their own float, ablaze with candles and flowers and bearing their Image. They each wear their own special uniform. Those of Jesus the Captive, who are all ex-prisoners, walk in white tunics and red hoods; those of Jesus the Nazarene in mulberry tunics and white hoods; those of the Virgin of Solitude in white tunics and black hoods; and so forth with the other *cofradias* from all over the city. The rearguard of all is the famous Christ of the Bull-fighters accompanied by matadors and novilleros. *Saetas* are sung at different points as the cortège slowly winds its way through the Calle de los Preciados, the Plaza de San Domingo, the Calle de San Bernardo, and down the Gran Vía to San José, where the *cofradias* disperse to their various churches and convents. By this time it is three o'clock in the morning.

The religious services take place, of course, in accordance with the Pontifical Decree of 1953 and the times can be found in the newspapers. *Tenebrae* is sung on Friday or Saturday morning, and on the night of Holy Saturday there are Masses in the churches, until at midnight the bells ring out to welcome Easter.

San Isidro

Madrid's own particular fiesta is that of San Isidro el Labrador on May 15th, which begins with the formal proclamation of the Saint from the balcony of the Panadería and then through the streets of the old town by gaily costumed heralds on horseback.

St. Isidore the Labourer was a humble Madrileño who should certainly be the patron saint of all of us who are idle and absentminded. A ploughman on the riverside farm of a nobleman called Juan de Vargas, he went to church one morning, forgot the time and was bawled out by his master for being late to work. They went together to the field and found two angels ploughing it for him. (Many a Madrileño since then has wished that he could find angels to do his work for him.) After his death he appeared with an unexpected burst of practicality to Alfonso VIII to guide his army to victory at Las Navas de Tolosa and deliver Andalusia. There can be little doubt that the wives of many saints have been 'walking saints' themselves, but very few have been officially canonised, as was the fortune of St. Isidore's wife, Santa María de la Cabeza, to make a sainted married couple.

On May 15th itself, there is a solemn Mass in the Cathedral, after which the Alcalde and other notables proceed to the saint's home in the Plaza de San Andrés to pray in the chapel. Thousands of people troop out to make the *romería* to the Pradera de San Isidro just beyond the river, where the saint's hermitage is situated. Although the pilgrimage has been less popular since the Communists used the Pradera as an execution ground, many Madrileños take picnic lunches and make a merry day of it, exactly as Goya has painted their great-grand-fathers, eating the traditional cakes called *rosquillos* and drinking wine, *anís* and beer leavened by the holy water of the hermitage, which is supposed to be very good for fever (although the sceptic might plump for boiled water). The day of the saint is crowned at midnight by a resplendent firework display at some open space such as the Plaza de Cibeles or the Plaza de Colón.

The whole fiesta lasts ten or eleven days. There is the football match of the year when Madrid plays Barcelona. There are athletics, basketball and pelota contests, polo tournaments, horse races, cycle races, motor races, jumping competitions, aeroplane competitions, swimming contests in the Retiro Lake and outboard motor races and water-skiing on the lake of the Casa del Campo, golf handicap competitions, dog shows, operas, symphony concerts, art exhibitions, shows of regional costumes, folk dances and marionettes—even prizes for illuminated shop-window displays.

Above all, there are eleven days of bullfights, starring the greatest matadors of Spain and tropical America. In the mornings, and more especially on the first Sunday morning before the fiesta, *aficionados* drive out to Las Ventas de Batán in the Casa de Campo to appraise and criticise the bulls which are to be fought. Each string is in its own separate corral, all the animals peacefully sleeping or chewing the cud and little dreaming of the wild and bloody battle which will in so few days put an end to their hitherto pampered lives. Just in front of the corrals is a restaurant-bar with a terrace where one can sit in the sun and ruminate back at the bulls. (Count no bull happy until it is dead, as Sophocles might have said!) From Batán the *aficionado* can go on to the bullring and watch the bulls destined to die that afternoon being sorted into their separate pens.

Popular rejoicings are laid on and fireworks crackle all over the town. The Plaza Mayor, its centre turned rather undignifiedly into a fairground with dodgems and hooplas and a large dance-floor, is ablaze with hundreds of Chinese lanterns, and all the streets leading down to the Barrios Bajos are illuminated with electric bulbs. The people dance in the streets until dawn. Every year at La Chopera in the Retiro or at La Corrala, an oblong open space in the Barrios Bajos between the Calles de Tribulete, Sombrerete and Mesón de Paredes, they stage one of those open-air operettas or *zarzuelas* which the Spaniards know how to do so well, such as *La Gran Vía* or *La Revoltosa*. The world-famous *La Verbena de la Paloma* had its première here in La Corrala.

Small wonder that Madrid used to be crowded with *isidros*, the nickname applied to the yokels who came up to gape at the shops, the lifts, the trams and the fashions, and were proverbially falling into the hands of grafters and slickers and getting lost and forgetting where they were staying. You still see many hayseeds up for the fiesta, but with the extension of local bus services Spanish villagers can now go into their local towns to see bull-fights and shops and trams, so that the *isidro* of tradition is becoming a thing of the past. Nowadays, to be candid, the true heirs of the *isidros* are the foreign businessmen and other 'visiting firemen' who generally seem to find that Madrid requires their presence urgently in the month of May and that no other time of the year will do. There are various annual magnets in Europe, such as Easter Week in Rome and Ascot Week in England, and San Isidro is one of them.

The Verbenas

The end of May brings the first of the *verbenas*, which go on all through the summer. The derivation of this word is as obscure as that of *tertulia*, although it seems to have something to do with the ancient belief that a lustration of water soaked in verbena was conducive to gaiety. *Verbenas* are popular fiestas attaching to the different quarters of Madrid, where they kill all sleep for a week or two. They consist generally of two parts, one an ordinary fair with all its accompaniments of swings, merry-go-rounds, distorting mirrors, flying cars and so forth, and the other of a *quermés* (the kermesse which the countrymen of Charles V brought to Spain in the sixteenth century) which is an open space for dances, elections of 'Misses', competitions and so forth every evening.

The opening *verbena* of the season is that of the Princesa quarter held in the Plaza de Moncloa near the Puerta de Hierro, but the first important one is that of San Antonio de la Florida on June 13th, which takes place in front of the twin churches down by the river in the Paseo de la Florida and in the open space known as La Bombilla. St. Antony of Padua is the patron saint of *grisettes* and seamstresses, and every year on the evening of June 12th the *modistillas* go down to San Antonio, dressed in the traditional Madrid costume, with a black shawl and a white headscarf, to pray and throw pins into the font to ask St. Antony for a husband.

Formerly they used to pray in the little round Ermita with the famous Goya frescoes, but that has now been secularised and turned into a museum in order to preserve the paintings from damage. In 1928 a replica was built next door and the image and cult transferred thither. It is perhaps a rather more suitable place for devotion than the remarkable little church designed by Villanueva in 1792 as the court chapel of Charles IV and in 1798 decorated, dome, spandrels and arches, by Goya, who is himself buried there. It is often described as his only important religious painting, but these frescoes are perhaps the most completely pagan paintings which ever decorated a Christian building (always and naturally excepting those at the Pauline convent at Parma which are little less than pornographic). Round the interior of the dome is a painted balustrade, with St. Antony preaching to a crowd which included portraits of some of the leading cocottes of the town, so that the aristocratic congregation had only to lift their eyes from their rosaries to meet those of their lovers of the night before. In the spandrels and arches, fleshy and fashionably, if rather scantily, dressed blonde angels are parting curtains of white and gold silk or reclining on their wings as though on pillows of swansdown. Decidedly no place for impressionable little shopgirls, one would think.

St. Antony's Fair goes on for a fortnight. There are races of waiters with trays and of men pushing handcarts with a girl on board, costume balls, parades of models, flamenco dancing, and, appropriately enough, a Queen of Couture, whose title was won one year that I remember by a girl who confectioned in a single night a dress with seven metres of stuff for a total cost of 74.50 pesetas. There are merry-go-rounds (which the Spaniards oddly call *tios vivos*, or 'live uncles'), shooting galleries, swings, flying cars and all the fun of the fair. Earthenware *botijos* circulate; barkers bark; *churro*-boilers steam and stench; the dust rises thick through the stink and the noise. Many people bring their own food and sit out in the cool of the evening in the *merenderos* by the river, which have tables and chairs and supply drinks. The last day of the fiesta, the second Sunday, is marked by a motor race in the Casa del Campo and a final ball or *quermés* which goes on until dawn.

In the old days the *verbenas* of St. John on June 23rd and St. Peter on June 28th were celebrated in the Prado. The former was a good example of co-existence, for the Moslems venerated St. John and celebrated his fiesta jointly with the Christians until their priests told them they offended Allah by consorting with unveiled women and dancing lascivious dances. Pérez Galdós describes these two fiestas as being very animated even in his time, but unfortunately the tradition has now been lost, like that of Santiago el Verde, Green St. James, the old spring festival on May Day.

The next *verbena* is that of Carmen on July 16th which is celebrated at Chamberí, although owing to the amount of traffic in that quarter the *quermés* has now been exiled to the open space in front of the New Ministries at the far end of the Paseo de la Castellana. Carmen is also the *verbena* of suburban Vallecas and Carabanchel.

Then in the long hot August nights the great *verbenas* of the Barrios Bajos crowd each other to overlapping—San Cayetano on the 7th, San Lorenzo on the 10th and Nuestra Señora de la Paloma on the 15th. Each is divided into two parts—the fair and the *quermés*. San Cayetano is the patron of Arganzuela with its *quermés* in La Corrala (beginning at eleven o'clock) and its fair in the Calle de

los Embajadores (so called because all the foreign am-
bassadors once fled there when there was a plague in
Madrid). There are competitions for decorated streets,
balconies, house fronts and patios and a procession of
giants and Bigheads, figures with fantastic papier-maché
masks like those of the Nice Carnival. Every night in
La Corrala there is a Great Ball; or a popular *zarzuela*;
or the elections of Queens and Misses with their maids of
honour, such as the Queen of the Andalusian Wine
Presses, Miss Metro, Miss Cotton, Miss Commerce and
the Arganzuela Girl; or a cotillon; or draws for dolls; or
parades of film starlets in evening dress. There are religious processions and services, fireworks, free meals for
children, purses for the aged poor, football matches,
gymkhanas, a circus, wrestling, boxing, a band concert,
a waiter's race and competitions for Manila shawls, for
mantillas and for combs.

San Lorenzo is the *verbena* of the Mediodía-Retiro
district. It has its fair in Lavapiés and its *quermés* in the
great open space in the Retiro Park called La Chopera.
Its various festivities are on the same lines as those of San
Cayetano. The church of San Lorenzo round which the
religious side centres is in Lavapiés, where the old Jewry
used to be, and is actually on the site of the synagogue.

The *verbena* of La Paloma on which Bretón de los
Herreros' operetta is based is the patronal fiesta of the
Latina quarter. Its fair is in the Rastro and its *quermés* in
the little park of Las Vistillas. The saint's day is on August
15th. Our Lady of the Dove is in fact the Assumption.
In addition to the other Misses (including curiously
enough Señoritas Casta y Susana, Chaste and Susanna),
Latina aspires to elect a Miss Spain (who has no connection

with London daily journalism). There are exhibitions of art and photography; a dance of *novios*, or engaged couples, with prizes; boys in sacks hunting a chicken; a greasy pole in the Calle de Rosario; 'Days' of the different Regions such as Andalusia, Estremadura and León. Five thousand people can gather in Las Vistillas to dance, refresh themselves and watch these varied spectacles. In addition, of course, there are the usual religious functions and gifts to the poor.

These *verbenas* in the slum quarters are among the gayest and most typical things which Madrid has to offer, and are not to be missed by anyone who has the misfortune to find himself in the city during August.

The autumn is a Lent-like lull. At All Souls the Madrileños go out to the cemeteries to visit their dead, and Zorrilla's play *Don Juán de Tenorio* is staged every November with the ritual punctuality of our own *Peter Pan* at Christmas.

In the days before Christmas turkeys are traditionally sold in the Plaza de Santa Cruz, and in the Plaza Mayor figures for the cribs called *Belenes* or Bethlehems which appear in churches and private houses. A forest of exotic northern Christmas trees suddenly covers the lawns of the Plaza de España. On Christmas Eve the boys go round beating saucepan lids, blowing whistles and shaking rattles, with the Puerta del Sol as ever the focus of the din.

Christmas Eve is a family festival. Cafés, restaurants, bars and even public transport shut down so that everyone can spend the evening at home with his family. So for this one evening in the year lonely men have to go to bed hungry and thirsty as well.

CHAPTER SIX

The Bullfighters' Quarter

In the old days it was proverbially impossible to move about Madrid without perpetually coming back to the Puerta del Sol, and this is largely true today, except for those who live their isolated lives out in the Castellana Hilton or the Palace Hotel or in the characterless new suburbs of the north and east. Thus we have to return there to start on our exploration of the seamier but, from the human point of view, most vital parts of Madrid which lie to the south of it.

The Calle del Principe leads down to the Plaza de Santa Ana with its little wine bars and pubs, and on the corner is a Galician bar-restaurant called O Pote, which is worth a visit for its shellfish. On another corner is the Villa Rosa where you can hire a private room and lay on a guitarist and singer for a *cuadro de flamenco*. The next street is the Calle de Victoria, where there are the official booking offices for the bullring. This street and the neighbouring ones, the Calle de la Cruz and the Calle de Espoz y Mina, are full of noisy little taverns bearing such taurine names as El Clarín, El Brindis, Sol y Sombra and La Oreja de Oro, with coloured Talavera tiles and stuffed bulls' heads on the walls. They are the hang-outs of all the hangers-on of the

D

bullring, endlessly arguing the finer points of tauro-machy.

There are several *casas de reventas* round here, ticket-brokers who buy tickets for bullfights, cinemas and football matches at a discount and sell them to the public at 20% over the price—a 20% which is worth paying as it saves endless queuing. On days when seats for the bulls are sold out, it is there that you go to find seedy-looking citizens offering black-market tickets at high prices.

It is in this quarter also that most of the taurine fan clubs have their headquarters. Many *aficionados* pay ten or twelve pesetas monthly to belong to one of these *peñas*, which generally has its seat in some tavern, al-though a few have their own club-houses. The largest of them is the Club Taurino Luís Miguel Domínguín with its social seat in the Carrera de San Jerónimo and a membership of some fifteen hundred. The monthly subscription is fifteen pesetas for original members and twenty-five for late comers plus one hundred pesetas entrance fee. Its club-rooms include a *salón* for *tertulias*, a bar, offices for the president and the secretary, and a library of books on tauromachy, all given by members. The walls are decorated with pictures, posters, pro-grammes and photographs of Luís Miguel Domínguín and with the heads of bulls killed by the master. Every October the club organises a series of lectures on complex and technical taurine problems by eminent authorities such as Don José María de Cossío, author of the monu-mental three-volume work *Los Toros*. It also organises banquets, fiestas and trips to see Luís Miguel fight.

Not far from the Ostrería in the Calle de la Cruz

which I have already mentioned, a popular little restaurant-bar is the Gayango at Calle de Nuñez de Arce 6, where they cook you a *parrillada* or mixed grill in alcohol on the table in front of you in an earthenware bowl. It also specialises in *pinchitos morros* on a skewer—a sort of *shish kebab* or *raznici*. The little bars of this quarter are well worth exploring if only for the sake of their habitués. The price of wine is such that one can carouse and pub-crawl the whole evening for a shilling or two.

Parallel to the Calle de Victoria is the Calle de Ventura de Vega, where there is a bullfighters' restaurant called Julián Rojo, well known not only for its typical dishes such as elvers and roast sucking-pig but for its fine collection of bullfighting photographs and pictures. Julián Rojo was a great friend of the painter Roberto Domingo and, when he died, bought forty of his paintings and a hundred of his drawings. He was also a friend of the great Manolete, who often dined here and in 1946 unbent so far as to dance flamenco here at the farewell party given him by his rival Arruza before his last tour in Mexico. If you speak Spanish and show you are an *aficionado*, Don Julián will talk bulls by the hour, take you on a tour round his walls, and show you his principal treasure, the green suit of lights in which Manolete was gored in Madrid in September 1943 and which he never wore again. (Pick it up and you will wonder how anybody could walk, let alone run with such a weight on him.) Don Julián has the last photograph of Manolete ever taken, and one of the few that show him smiling, on that fatal August afternoon when he was killed in Linares and all Spain went into mourning. On the wall is the head of the bull which I saw Litri kill at the Feria de San Isidro in 1957 and which earned him two ears, an award almost unprecedented in the Madrid ring up till then.

Parallel with the Calle de Ventura de Vega is the Calle de Echegaray, lined with little bars, eating shops and honky-tonks. In the old days this used to be the rowdiest street in Madrid, full of drunks and trollops. Now it has been cleaned up, but there is still some chance of seeing a little fun or fighting on a Saturday evening.

A Wineshop in the Barrios Bajos

Further on, where the Barrios Bajos proper begins, in the narrow bustling seventeenth-century street of Calle de Mesón de Paredes (which leads from the Plaza de Tirso de Molina down to Lavapiés), a coach-lamp hangs over the door of Number Thirteen. It marks the tavern of Antonio Sánchez, one-time *matador de toros*, a long, dark, narrow room, buzzing with voices and thick with tobacco smoke. It has old bullfighting posters and pictures on its smoke-blackened walls, but none of the usual football posters of other taverns, for 'where the portraits of Frascuelo and Lagartijo adorn the walls, there will be no men in shorts,' says Don Antonio firmly.

In the outer bar is the head of Fogonero, the bull killed by our host when he took his alternative from the ill-fated Sánchez Mejías, for he was one of the leading matadors of Spain until one afternoon in 1929 a right-hooking bull ignored his *muleta*, went straight for his body and ripped him up so badly that it was eight years before he could think of returning to the ring. By then he was too old to do so and took over his father's wineshop in the Barrios Bajos, over which he had been born. The inner room, where the local people bring their food wrapped in newspaper to eat with the wine of the house, is hung with his own pictures, for he has taught himself to become a fine portrait painter and works in his studio every morning when he is not instructing in the bull-fighting school at Vista Alegre.

If you see a very slight, very distinguished-looking figure with a nut-brown face and snow-white hair, wearing a black broadcloth suit and perhaps a stiff black Cordoba hat, that is your host. Indeed, you may perhaps have already recognised him from the famous portrait by his friend Ignacio Zuloaga which now hangs in the Zuloaga Museum at Zumaya near San Sebastian and which first aroused the young *torero*'s interest in painting.

Like Don Julián Rojo he will be happy to sit and talk bulls and lament the old days when bulls were big and *toreros* were brave. It will cost you little to invite him to a drink, for his excellent white wine is only a penny a glass or tenpence a bottle.

'I only sell wine, not meals. I have kept the place exactly as my father left it to me,' says Don Antonio, adding, like the true Spaniard he is, 'no doubt I should make more money if I brought it up to date, but then I should have no time to see all the bullfights, nor to go to the country, nor to paint in my studio, and for what time remains to me of life those are the things I want to do.'

You can see a typical old Madrid wineshop without trailing all the way to the Barrios Bajos, by visiting the Bodega Alvarez in the picturesquely named Calle de

Valgamedíos, or Bless-my-soul Street, north of the
Gran Vía, with its smoke-browned walls and the great
round barrels with their tops worn and chipped by the
many thousands of glasses placed on them over the long
and thirsty decades. In the owner's private parlour is the
usual *tertulia* of his regulars and personal friends. But,
just as the cafés have been supplanted by the cafeterias,
and the old *figones* by restaurants, so the wineshops are
being replaced by stand-up bars where youths drink
Coca-Cola and queue to play the penny-in-the-slot
football game called *futbolín*.

Drink

In the bars and wineshops of the Barrios Bajos and the
poorer quarters generally, a glass of ordinary wine costs
a penny or two, a glass of sherry about threepence, and a
glass of brandy sixpence. The cheap *vino corriente* of the
taverns formerly came from Arganda in the Province of
Madrid but now it has largely been replaced by Toledo
wine. Málaga wine is little drunk in Madrid; the usual
apéritif wine is sherry, a term technically confined to
wines from the district of Jeréz de la Frontera. (You ask
for a *chato*, which is a sherry glass, or for a *fino*; if you
want it very dry ask for a *jeréz seco* which is none other
than Falstaff's 'Sherris Sack'.) A good place for the
connoisseur of sherry is the Bar Jeréz in the Calle de
Valdeiglesias, where the Gran Vía runs into the Alcalá,
which has barrels of *finos*, *olorosos* and *soleras* for the
visitor to experiment with at will. Good dry sherries little
known in England are San Patricio, La Ina and Viña

AB. Whether it is a matter of the altitude or not, it is my experience that one cannot drink more than two or three sherries in Madrid. (Sherry is fortified only for export— not for the Peninsula itself.) They need treating with some respect in any case. While the very light sherries might be imagined to be innocuous, they are in fact the most livery of all. A fairly innocent friend of mine arrived in Madrid for the first time and on his first evening drank a bottle and a half of equally innocent-seeming *manzanilla*. He was in bed for two days as a result. The very dry light *manzanilla* comes from San Lúcar de Barrameda, near the mouth of the Guadalquivir. Sweeter and rather heavier are *moriles* and *montilla* from the Province of Cordoba. Genuine port is very expensive and as hard to find as sherry in Portugal, although there is a Galician substitute called *Bandeira*.

These are all aperitives or dessert wines. The best-known table wines are the Rioja from the Province of Logroño (with Riscal, Murrieta and Lasala among the best vintages) and the Valdepeñas from La Mancha; they constitute the usual *vino corriente* of a Madrid restaurant. Both of these are considered to come better in their red than in their white versions, but there is a very fine white wine from Valladolid called Vega Sicilia, which is well worth the attention of a connoisseur who is prepared to pay anything over a pound a bottle.

In summer, when straight wine seems too heavy, many people drink *sangría*, a 'cup' made of wine diluted with soda water, lemon and ice. It goes down the throat very quickly and easily and is rather headier than it seems, especially on a summer afternoon.

The sage advice 'Never drink spirits in Spain' is a

half-truth like so many pieces of good advice, and is ambiguous because the English language lacks the two 'aspects' of the Slavonic verb. It should be interpreted not as 'Never touch spirits in Spain', for almost anything in this world can be done occasionally, but 'Never make a habit of drinking spirits in Spain', for if you do they will make you ill much quicker than in England.

The smart bars sell mainly whisky, gin and vermouth. Spanish gin is quite adequate for gin fizzes and cocktails and is harmless when taken in moderation. It is, of course, much cheaper than imported English gin. A gin and vermouth is called a *combinación*.

Spanish brandy, at about five shillings a bottle, is a different drink altogether from French brandy, but a *copa* or *copita* (which is what you ask for) makes a good short drink and there are excellent liqueur brandies for post-prandial use such as Felipe Segundo, Carlos Primero and, my own preference, Larios 1866. But let no one delude himself that, as he cannot afford his customary ration of whisky and soda, which runs to about seven shillings a tot, Spanish brandy and soda will serve as a substitute; taken regularly and in any quantity, it is very hard on the liver and apt to cause that distressing form of palsy known as 'the shakes'.

As a short drink, brandy's great rival is *anís*, of which there are two kinds, the sweet Anís del Mono (you can go over the distillery at Chinchón in Madrid Province) and the dry Anís de Clavel, which is more like the Italian *grappa* or the German *Schnapps*. A *sol y sombra* consists of equal parts of brandy and *anís*. As a long drink to stand in for brandy and soda, I have found that one can last an evening on Bacardi rum and soda without any ill effects to follow, but to a non-Caribbean the taste is rather sickly. A popular drink is a *Cuba Libre*, which is rum and Coca-Cola. All drinks in Madrid are doubles unless otherwise stated. If you want a small one you ask for a 'half'—for example, *una media combinación* or 'half a combination'.

Owing to Spanish restrictions on imports there is hardly a liquor in the world which is not made under licence in Catalonia; Bacardi and Negrita rum, Pernod, Marie Brizard, Campari and Cinzano vermouth, Dubonnet, Fernet Branca, Curaçao, Cointreau, Kümmel, Kirsch, Marasquino—and now even whisky is being matured for sale in Segovia. As in the case of the scents and the deodorants likewise made under licence in Barcelona, comparison with the originals leads one to suspect a strong admixture of H_2O but at least (unlike some of the Middle Eastern whiskies) they do not appear to have acquired any actively noxious ingredients.

The technique of drinking at a bar is different from ours. Thus the silly and pernicious round-for-round rule does not operate. If you invite a Spaniard to a drink he will seldom stand you one back again even if you encourage him by ordering another round yourself, but the next time you meet him he will probably offer you one and if you try to buy him the other half he will refuse and order two more with some remark such as 'I am in the chair this evening'. But in general friends meeting at a bar buy their own drinks or shoot dice for them and do not invite each other to rounds. If you do stand a round it is manners not to ask your companion what he will have but to address the barman directly: '*Yo invito al señor*' or '*Invito a los señores*'. Remember that it is very

unlucky to invite anyone to a 'last drink', for that means
the last drink they will have on earth. It is always the
'penultimate' drink. In a *tasca* one does not tip; in a smart
bar leave a peseta for a single drink or up to five if you
have been having several *penultimatos*.

Tapas, the equivalent of the Greek *mezes*, are always
served with a drink. In smart bars they are generally
almonds, monkey-nuts, popcorn, olives or *rancheritos*,
which are tiny little Catherine wheels made of flour; in
the *tascas* an anchovy, a potato chip, a prawn, or a bit of
smoked ham or fried fish. Always take the *tapa* whether
you want it or not, for it is considered barbarous to drink
without eating. Spaniards call it '*beber como un flamenco*'—
drinking like a Fleming—or, as the famous Chinaman
said, 'Me dlinkee for dlunkee'.

Beer is becoming increasingly popular in Madrid.
Spanish beers are all of the kind we should describe as a
light lager, except for one brand of black beer. Guinness
can be had in a very few places. The draught beer
(*cerveza a granel*) is on the whole better than the bottled—
especially in the early part of the day. Excellent for
'elevenses', it has a tendency, so connoisseurs say, to go
off a bit in the evening. It is drawn from the tap in any
of the *cervecerías* or beer-shops but not as a rule in cafés
or bars. The usual measures are a *caña*, which is officially
two hundred grams or a fifth of a litre, and a *doble* which
is two-fifths, but you can also get a 'pony' or *corta*, which
is half a *caña*, or a *tercio*, which is a third of a litre.

Spain is a hard country for a teetotaller, for wine costs
considerably less than mineral water and is a fraction of
the price of such non-alcoholic substitutes as *horchata*,
Coca-Cola or fruit juice. There are good straight fruit

and tomato juices on the market, but avoid the cheap *gaseosas* called *limonada* or *naranjada* which are merely chemicals with bubbles put into them. Be sure to ask for *zumo* or *jugo* of whatever fruit it is you want. Fruit shakes are called *batidos*. There is also a non-alcoholic fruit cocktail oddly called a *veriwell*, which the smarter bars can produce for teetotal clients or for those who think it is too early in the day to start drinking—which it generally is, considering how late everything goes on in Madrid.

The three local mineral waters are the still Solares and the slightly fizzy Insalus and Vichy Catalán, but it is not really necessary to order them, since the local water is among the purest and best-flavoured in the world and is really a pleasure to drink. It is piped down from the Lozoya reservoir in the Sierra de Guadarrama to the reservoirs in northern Madrid. Be careful about putting ice in it, as that can have collected dirt on the way.

The Rastro

The slum quarters of the Barrios Bajos run down south through what was once the ghetto to the Plaza de Lavapiés, whose name of Washfeet recalls one of the many old fountains of Madrid. Round to the right is the flea market or *Rastro* which is held daily in the Ribera de los Curtidores and which got its name because in the old days it was the only place where the tanners were allowed to ply their malodorous trade. Sunday morning is the time to go for bargains, and the earlier the better. Most of the stuff is junk, but there are some good antique shops in the two courts, the Galerías Piquer on the left and the Nuevas Galerías on the right. In one of them I have been offered a rather dubious El Greco for four hundred thousand pesetas. At the top is the Plaza de Cascorro and to the west of it is the Plaza de Vara del Rey with more antique shops. The baroque saints and angels and cherubim seemed to me expensive and rather dubious both as to quality and to authenticity. An enormous number of these objects were burnt or chopped up all over Spain in 1936 and ever since the priests have been trying to find replacements, so that genuine bargains are not easily come by.

Beyond the Plaza is the principal street of the Barrios Bajos, the Calle de Toledo, in which that conscientious chronicler Pérez Galdós once counted no fewer than eighty-eight taverns. It runs down from St. Isidore's Cathedral to the Toledo Gate, where the wholesale fish market is. It is no good trying to combine lunch at María Aroca's with a Sunday morning in the Rastro, for she shuts on Sundays.

One of the streets beyond the Calle de Toledo is among the most *folclorico* survivals of Madrid. The Cava Baja was originally an underground gallery made by the Moors for getting in and out of Madrid in time of need, with its exit below the Puerta de Moros. When the Christians took Madrid, the Moors and their families crept out through this tunnel with what they could carry of their possessions. Later it became the rendezvous for all the carters and muleteers coming into town from beyond the Manzanares. It was lined with old coaching inns, several of which still survive. Some of the local bus lines and carriers from Toledo way still use the old

ALVAREZ ORTEGA

El Rastro

posadas and *paradores* as their Madrid terminals and one, the Mesón del Segoviano, formerly the Posada de San Pedro, functions as a restaurant. It is a reeking, smoke-blackened place, much appreciated by tourists for its 'atmosphere'. It should not be confused with the Mesón de San Javier, another very typical *tasca* of old Madrid in 'the Labyrinth' down behind the Ayuntamiento and, the morbid may care to know, almost opposite the old Inquisition building.

CHAPTER SEVEN

The Academy

We now find ourselves back again at the Plaza del Sol as though at the centre of a maze and while we draw breath we can snatch a moment to look at the dignified Charles III buildings on the left of the Alcalá before the banks begin like frozen circuses to display their elephants and chariots and naked strong men. The first palace is Sabatini's old Customs House, now the Ministry of Finance, and the second is the Academia de Bellas Artes de San Fernando, with a façade by Villanueva. The Royal Academy of Noble Arts of St. Ferdinand was originally dedicated to painting, sculpture and architecture. When music was added, it became the Royal Academy of Beautiful Arts, music presumably being beautiful without being noble.

The collection it contains is so small that it can easily be combined with an exploration of the Sol quarter, but with the Prado, the Armoury and the Lázaro-Galdiano Museum it is one of the four Madrid 'musts' for the art-lover on account of the pictures assembled there from destroyed convents and from Godoy's collection. There are a number of Goya portraits, including the Godoy and the famous self-portrait, and five of his most important subject pictures, *The Madhouse*, *The Inquisition*, *The*

Flagellants, The Bullfight and *The Burial of the Sardine*. There are also a series of powerful portraits of Merce-darian monks by Zurbarán, a remarkable Pereda, and a number of early nineteenth-century portraits by Vicente López and others, which lose most of their interest through not being labelled.

San Jerónimo

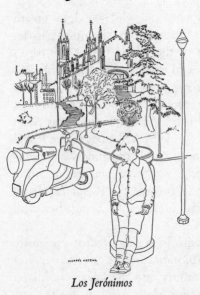

Los Jerónimos

From the Puerta del Sol, Madrid spreads east along another road beside the Alcalá, for Philip II took a fancy to the Mona-stery of San Jerónimo on the little hill behind the Prado, where now stands the rebuilt Gothic church of that name. Access from Madrid was by way of the Carrera de San Jerónimo running parallel to the Alcalá on the south. It is now a busy street of shops, which include not only Lhardy's the pastrycook but the Casa del Fumador, where you can actually get a pipe mended.

Tobacco

'The Spanish exiles smoking their little paper cigars' were a source of wonderment to the English writers of a century ago, and the inventors of the cigarette are still heavy and inveterate smokers. They consume in a year one thousand eight hundred million ready-rolled cigarettes besides two hundred and forty million packets of tobacco (*picadura*) and eighty-eight million cigars. Undaunted by minatory notices, they smoke on inflammable film sets, when peering into your petrol tank at a filling station, in operating theatres—everywhere, in fact, except in churches and cinemas, which, oddly enough, are two of the most crowded places in any Spanish town.

Ready-rolled cigarettes are now common enough but many Spaniards still buy tobacco and paper separately and roll their own cigarettes—an art not easy for a butter-fingered foreigner to master. Most Spanish cigarettes are made of black tobacco. The most popular brand made of *tabaco rubio*, as the Spaniards call Virginia-type tobacco, is the Bisonte, quite smokeable and much cheaper than the Chesterfields which are made in Spain from imported American leaf. The cheapest of the black-tobacco cigarettes are the Ideales (Caldo de Gallina), which are not made up. If you want them ready rolled ask for *Ideales de dos diez*, so called because they retail—or used to—at 2.10 pesetas. Rather better are the Peninsulares at 2.50. English cigarettes are not on sale at the tobacco monopoly shops or *estancos*, but are sold quite openly by the black-marketeers, generally buxom,

weatherbeaten old women who sit about at the main
street-corners. As they are all of them smuggled—the
cigarettes, not the old women—they are naturally priced
accordingly.

Recently the Monopoly placed a pipe tobacco on the
market, which is not bad if you like the sweet, dry,
quick-smoking American type. English pipe-tobacco is
practically unprocurable unless you have a very smart
bootlegger with contacts in Gibraltar or one of the ports.
But a pound of English tobacco will always be allowed
through the Customs, and one can always stretch one's
supply by mixing it with the local product.

Since the importation of Havana cigars was prohibited
in 1959 to save foreign currency, the only *puros*, as the
Spaniards call cigars, are those grown in the Canary
Islands. The best-known brands are called Belleza and
Rumba. The flavour is good but they tend to come
unrolled in your mouth. There are also, of course, all
kinds of cheap black stoogies smoked with relish by the
locals. If you want to try one, ask for a *faria*. It is not
nearly as fierce as it looks.

The Cortes

The Carrera de San Jerónimo debouches into the Plaza
de los Cortes. Antique dealers and souvenir shops cluster
here and in the adjacent Calle del Prado, lured no doubt
by the proximity of the touristful Palace Hotel (which
claims to be the largest in Europe). Here tourists too
hurried to go out to Toledo can at least buy the products
of that ancient city. Its swords, for example, have long

Fuente de Apolo

been among the most famous in the world and are so
finely tempered that they can be bent double in a complete circle. The steel comes from Eibar near Bilbao,
which is why a Toledo blade was called by Shakespeare
and his contemporaries a 'bilbo'.

For those who do not want to buy a sword (and not
everybody does nowadays), there are cigarette-cases,
powder-boxes, penknives, scissors, brooches, cuff-links,
and a hundred and one other trinkets of damascened
Toledo work. The inlay is of fine gold wire hammered
into tiny channels and holes already made on the black
metal. All Toledo rings like an Oriental bazaar with the
hammer of the inlaying and the forging of swords.

To the left of the Plaza, in the Calle de Zorrilla, are
several foreign restaurants. The German Edelweiss, often
known simply as '*los Alemanes*', is like the Piamontesa in
the Costanilla de los Angeles, cheap and so popular with
tourists that you should go at a quarter past one or before
nine to be certain of a table; the Gambrinus, which is
Austrian; and the Heidelberg which, like the Baviera, is
now German in name and decoration only. To the right
is the quiet, decayed, once literary, quarter where
Cervantes, Lope de Vega and Quevedo lived. In the Calle
de Moratín there is a restaurant called La Hoja, which the
members of the French Embassy are reputed to frequent
(but perhaps that is just clever publicity).

Beyond the Palace Hotel are the Champs Elysées of
Madrid, the wide tree-shaded avenue with four pave-
ments and three carriage ways which runs for some five
miles through the city, changing aliases all the way—
Paseo de Atocha, Paseo del Prado, Salón del Prado,
Paseo de los Recoletos (otherwise Calvo Sotelo), Paseo de

la Castellana, and finally Avenida del Generalísimo. An English friend, arriving for the first time, said she had never imagined that Madrid was so like Paris.

With its magnolia trees, its rose gardens, its flower beds and its fountains, it is more like a garden than a street. There are three fountains in the single short stretch of the Salón del Prado, the Cibeles in the Plaza de Cibeles, featuring a matronly Cybele drawn in a chariot by lions, which is impressive when flood-lit; the Neptune showing the god sitting on a scallop shell drawn by sea-horses and assisted apparently by paddle wheels—and Ventura Rodríguez's Apollo. If there is a slight touch of absurdity about the Cybele and the Neptune, the Apollo at least can be admired without reserve. In front of the Neptune is the Palace Hotel and behind it the Ritz; below it is Villanueva's Prado Museum and beyond that again the Botanical Gardens which stretch right down to Atocha.

In the old fifteenth-century monastery of San Jerónimo the kings had suites permanently reserved for mourning and retreats (*retiros*) until eventually Philip IV, cuckoo-fashion, annexed the entire place and converted it into the Palace of El Retiro, leaving the monks and the monastery embedded in a corner of it. The only surviving pieces of the palace now are the Military Museum and the Museum of Plaster Casts, whose main hall is the old throne-room with Luca Giordano's fine painting of *The Triumph of the Golden Fleece* on the ceiling.

Parks

The great park of El Retiro, which the King took over
with the monastery and which was presented to the city
in 1876, is one of the most attractive in Europe. Among
the fine cedars of Lebanon and other trees are statues,
fountains and sculptures, kiosks, bars and chairs. There
is even a little open-air lending library and on the other
side of the Paseo de Coches is the Madrid Zoo. In the
summer boys come around hawking *barquillos*, which are
large, tasteless, folded-over wafers. In the middle of the
park is an artificial lake and on its promenade, the Salón
del Estanque, lonely people come with bits of bread to
make friends with the goldfish and watch the inexpert
oarsmen catching crabs, while nursemaids in picturesque
regional costumes while away their hours of pram-
watching by flirting with the soldiers. (On army pay of
half a peseta a day there is little to do but flirt with
chachas.) In summer there are two open-air restaurants,
the Florida and the Pabellón.

The Parterre opposite the Calle Maura Gate was laid
out by Philip II in honour of his wife and first cousin
once removed, Mary Tudor of England, who never saw
it. Some of the Retiro statues are remarkable. An over-
flow to the kings of the Plaza del Oriente and the
Parterre, there is a whole avenue here of surplus Spanish
monarchs once destined to man the Palace roof. The
profiles of their consorts are depicted in bas-relief on their
shields. Notice the finely imitated lacework and frills in
stone on the robe of Maria Luisa of Savoy, the homesick
little queen of Philip IV, who gave its name to the

district of Chamberí because for some unfathomable reason it reminded her of her own little mountain capital. Not all the statues are so well preserved, however, and the first two Charles's in particular look especially gruesome without their noses.

The most unexpected statue in the park is that of the Fallen Angel. One imagines that in all the world it must be the solitary memorial to Lucifer. Be that as it may, it is a strangely Manichean monument to come across in the land of the Inquisition, which was founded to stamp out that very heresy in Western Europe.

Going on past Piquer's Fallen Angel one finds oneself in front of the magnificent rose garden, one of the two great *rosaledas* in Madrid. It now has a rival in the Parque del Oeste at the bottom of the hill in front of the Paseo de Rosales, which was planted and opened some three years ago. In the spring, when the blooms are out, it provides three acres of vivid magnificent colour. One of the first things which the stranger will notice about the Parque del Oeste is that all the trees are very young. In fact the park was in the front line for three years during the siege of Madrid and not a tree survived. It was like a First-World-War picture of the Somme. When the young poplars and acacias have grown up it should make nearly as beautiful a park for western Madrid as the Retiro for eastern. From here there are pleasant walks along the banks of the Manzanares and many *gatos* bring their *novias* on a fine Sunday afternoon.

The Plaza de Cibeles

Formerly the Retiro stretched right down to the Salón del Prado as far as the Plaza de Cibeles, but a part has been built over to form the so-called Greek Quarter, which prides itself on being the quietest and most distinguished part of Madrid. Indeed, the Plaza de Cibeles, where the Alcalá, the Paseo de los Recoletos and the Salón del Prado meet, now has some claim to have replaced the Puerta del Sol as the centre of gravity of modern Madrid. The General Post Office, the War Office, and the Bank of Spain and the Transmediterranean Shipping Company occupy three of its four corners. The Stock Exchange, the Ministry of Marine and three or four of the de luxe hotels are within a short walk. Two of the expensive international restaurants to which business men invite each other on their expense accounts are in the nearby Calle de Alfonso XII, Horcher's and the Alabraso (the other two, apart from the hotels, are the Jockey, pronounced 'Hockey', in the Calle de Amador de los Rios, and the Bellman in the Calle de Madrazo). The Plaza is flanked by the aristocratic Barrio Griego, Serrano and Salamanca quarters. It has several open-air cafés and the kiosks with the widest selection of foreign newspapers in the capital.

Newspapers

The London papers arrive on the kiosks at about 7.30 in the evening of the same day or 1.30 in the afternoon on the morrow, because on certain days of the week the

Cibeles

airlines run a snob service which does not carry newspapers. The Sunday papers are not released until Monday
evening, as the Spanish censorship takes a day off on
Sundays. While there is no censorship upon the outgoing
messages of foreign correspondents, there is a censorship
upon incoming newspapers. This means that the English
papers will mysteriously disappear from the kiosks for
days at a time (as, for example, when the Spanish
Ambassador was cited in a divorce case)—which is why
a friend of mine once wrote to the editor of the London
daily to which he subscribed asking him not to print any
Spanish news until the Test matches were over.

Spanish papers run to rather peremptory-sounding
monosyllabic names. You can buy one by shouting 'Ya'
in Madrid or 'Hoy' in Seville—snappier titles, to give them
their due, than For a Lasting Peace and a People's Demo-
cracy. No paper can scoop another. The news as such is
much the same in all three Madrid morning papers, but
the emphasis is often different. A.B.C. is monarchist and
splashes royal weddings and the movements of the
Pretender and his family; Ya is the clerical organ and
gives a front page spread to all the pronouncements of
the Pope; while the Falangist Arriba goes to town on the
anniversaries of José Antonio and suchlike events.

The clerical Ya is the only one made up in the English
style and is therefore the easiest one for picking out the
news. A.B.C. is bound up (when they bother to staple it
together at all) like a weekly review and it is not easy to
find one's way about. The news begins about a third of
the way through, after the magazine section, whose
excellent articles and stories, especially in the Sunday
edition, constitute the only serious reading of millions of

Spaniards. It carries the most nearly objective political commentaries and has the best foreign correspondents, who give a very fair view of what is happening in London, Paris and Washington; it also employs Mingote, one of the wittiest black and white artists in Europe and one of the few men in Spain who can criticise the authorities and get away with it. Like all Spanish papers its treatment of foreign names is cavalier in the extreme. My favourite cutting from it relates to the Oman revolt of 1957, when, after reporting for several days the despatch of a detachment of the 'Cameroon Highlanders', a helpful sub-editor short of a line explained that they came from the British Cameroons. I also liked the occasion when, according to *A.B.C.*, the U.S.A. was represented at the late Pope's funeral by its former Ambassador to the Quirinal, 'Mrs. Boot Lace'.

Of the four evening papers, *Pueblo* is the organ of the Government-run Trade Unions; *Informaciones* belongs to a Traditionalist, that is to say Carlist, group, and *Madrid* and *Alcázar* to independent but, of course, pro-Government proprietors. The daily papers come out on Sunday but not on Monday. On Monday appears a sheet called *La Hoja de Lunes* produced by the Press Association. The most popular paper in Madrid, to judge by the number of people reading it, is the sporting daily, *Marca*.

Nuestra Señora de las Comunicaciones

The Central Post Office, built in 1911, has been considerably reconstructed after the Civil War, in which, as the centre of the Republic's communications with the outside world, it received no fewer than a hundred and fifty-five direct hits. It is an ornate piece of 'neo-baroque', whose heavy pinnacled roof looked to Ramón Gómez de la Serna as though Providence were playing a giant game of chess upon it. Innumerable plump pigeons make their homes in the deep recesses of its façade (a survival of the traditional connection between pigeons and posts?) and strut up and down the pavement in front of the main door, where tiny children are shown how to feed them so as to be photographed with them and their doting parents by the ambulant photographers. There are ancient crones proffering black-market cigarettes and others crying lottery tickets; men hawk budgerigars, which are carried perched on poles and are perpetually escaping and running off along the pavement to join the pigeons. The whole scene is very gay. There are no shops here. The draws are the out-of-door cafés and beershops, the sunshine and the view, the newspaper kiosks, the pigeons, the bootblacks, and above all the General Post Office, to which so many people have to go to collect parcels and for a hundred other reasons.

On the side of the Palacio de los Correos facing the Salón del Prado are a number of letter boxes bearing such labels as 'Canarias' and 'Barcelona'. Posting directly in these boxes will often save you a post, as will the purchase of an extra stamp marked *Urgente*. If you are posting to England, the *buzón* which interests you is the one marked 'Avion'. All letters to England go automatically by air for six pesetas, so there is no point in wasting money on an air mail stamp. Besides the post office, stamps (*sellos de correos*) can be bought in any of the *estancos*, little shops or kiosks generally identifiable from afar by their red and yellow stripes, which sell tobacco and other state monopolies.

The General Post Office has, of course, a Poste Restante counter, which in Spanish is labelled *Lista de Correos*, at the far end on the right in the entresol. It is a very useful address when you do not know exactly where you will be. I used to employ it too when I stayed just outside a little town near Alicante. Pedro the Postman had told a friend of mine: 'Of course, *señora*, I only bring your letters all the way out here because I happen to like you', and I did not know whether or not he would take a liking to me as well. Pigeonhole 67 on the left of the entresol exists for the benefit of stamp-collectors.

When telephoning you give the numbers in pairs; thus for 390457 you say *treinte y nueve—zero cuatro—cincuenta y siete*. To reply, answer melodramatically '*Dígame!*'—'Say to me!' Public call-boxes, generally in cafés, bars or shops, carry outside the sign of a white telephone on a black background, and to use them you buy a *ficha* or disc from the bar or shop assistant.

Useful numbers to know are:

Fire	474700
Police	216516
The Exact Time	093
Information	003
Long-distance call	009
International	008
Radio Taxis	312800

Remember that Spanish servants have never been known to get a foreign name even remotely right, so if your contact is out it is useless to leave a message unless you have prearranged a code-name such as 'José' or 'Señor Fernández'. The alternative is to spell out each letter according to the Spanish equivalent of our 'Abel—Baker—Charlie—Don'. Thus I am understood if I leave my name as Señor Lérida Yuste Antonio Llobregat. The following recognised list is well worth memorising or pasting up beside your telephone. Especially as it will enable you to send telegrams in English through a Hispanoglot operator.

A —Antonio
B —Barcelona
C —Carmen
CH—Chocolate (pronounce the 'e')
D —Dinamarca
E —España
F —Francia
G —Gerona (G as h)
H —Historia (the 'h' is mute)
I —Italia
J —Jeréz ('J' as 'h')
K —Kilo
L —Lérida
LL —Llobregat
M—Madrid
N—Navarra
O—Oviedo
P—París
Q—Querido
R—Roma
S—Sevilla
T—Toledo
U—Ubeda (accent on the U)
V—Valladolid
W—Washington
X—Xiquena (as in 'chicanery')
Y—Yuste
Z—Zaragoza

CHAPTER EIGHT

The Alcalá Gate

Up the Alcalá, looking eastward from the Plaza de Cibeles, along the road by which everything, kings and queens, war and peace and progress, has come to Madrid, is the triumphal arch which Sabatini erected for King Charles III in 1778, where the cherubs and trophies in snowy Colmenar limestone settle lightly on the grey Guadarrama granite like great white butterflies. Beyond it on the right is the entrance to the Retiro and on the left the Calle de Serrano and the beginning of the Salamanca Quarter. Between them the long, dusty road starts its journey across mountain and plain to Barcelona and Paris and Rome and Vienna.

The Salamanca Quarter

In the middle of the last century Madrid still consisted only of the six thousand six hundred and seventy cramped old houses of the centre, when a daring and energetic banker named Don José Salamanca conceived the idea of building a new upper-class suburb with wide streets and high uniform houses on the Parisian model. In 1872 he obtained a concession to acquire land and lay out his suburb just outside the Puerta de la Independencia on the north side of the Retiro and the Alcalá. His new quarter consisted of twenty-eight right-angled streets of international standards of comfort although of an un-exampled ugliness—the first 'European' extension of what the Spanish Balzac, Pérez Galdós called a 'dilapi-dated, dirty, inconvenient, disorderly and dark town'.

Apart from architecture and town-planning, the Sala-manca Quarter has exerted a perceptible sociological influence, for eighty years of living side by side, going to school together and intermarrying between the children of the lesser nobility and of the moneyed middle and professional classes who settled in the South Kensington of Madrid has bred a so-called 'Salamanca class' of liberal gentry which hardly existed before. If the main street *in* the quarter is the wide Calle de Velázquez with its two modern luxury hotels, the Velázquez and the Wellington (the only public mention of the Duke I have been able to discover in the length and breadth of Spain), it is not too much to say that the main street *of* the quarter is the Calle de Serrano, which forms its western boundary.

On sunny days, the elegant teenagers of the Salamanca and 'Embassy' Quarters sip their Coca-Colas in the out-door cafés of the Castellana, but when they graduate to the vermouth age they move over to the cafés and bars of the Calle de Serrano such as the Roma, the Xauen, the Garbi and the Manila. There before luncheon, between twelve and two, and especially on Sundays after Mass, the pretty little *Serranitas* may be seen flirting discreetly and making dates with their swains for the cinemas and thé-dansants in the afternoon. Their jealous elders nickname them *topolinos* and *topolinas*.

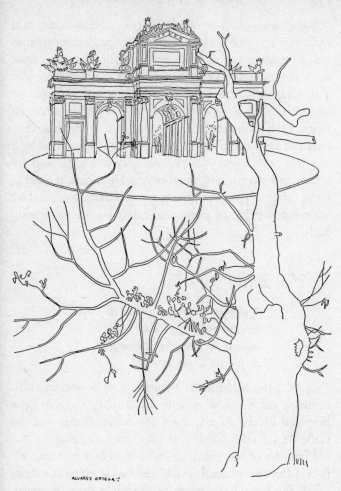

ALVAREZ ORTEGA

Puerta de Alcalá

E

Some way out beyond the Barrio de Salamanca and built two or three decades later is a second experiment in town-planning for the moneyed middle class, this time for those in search of open air and a semi-country life. The Ciudad Lineal is perhaps the earliest example of organised ribbon development. It is a single street of villas, each with its little garden, and is no less than twenty kilometres long. This tapeworm is vitalised by a bus line which runs the whole way along it, and by sewers and electric and water mains. Doubtless, it was the latest thing in 1900 but now it wears a shabby-genteel air little relieved by an occasional nightclub or swimming bath.

The Bulls

Quién no ha visto en tarde de toros
nuestra calle de Alcalá
aunque de la vuelta al mundo,
de fijo no la verá.

In 1872 the Marqués de Salamanca, as he was by then, rounded off his new quarter by buying the site now bounded by the Alcalá, the Calle de Velázquez and the Calle de Claudio Coello, at that time occupied by the old bullring of Madrid. Originally built by Ferdinand VI, it held eleven thousand people and had seen the triumphs of all the legendary heroes of the early days, Romero, Costillares and Pepe Hillo, who was killed here in 1801, right down to Frascuelo and Lagartijo.

Perhaps the most dramatic moment of its history was on the summer afternoon when the *toril* door opened for the first bull of the day and out rocketed a friar, hotly pursued by the bull and narrowly saved by the astonished capemen. Fray Martín, a keen *aficionado* like so many of his cloth, had been watching the *apartado*, or penning of the bulls, that morning when, unnoticed by anyone, he overbalanced and fell into the *corral*. He fled into the half-dark *toril*, whence the bulls are let out for their last journey, and saved himself by keeping absolutely motionless and hardly daring to breathe during the long hours before the fight began.

Another spectacular incident occurred in 1929 when a bull escaped from the second Madrid bullring during the *descajonamiento*, when the bulls were being released from their travelling boxes, and trotted all the way up the Alcalá to its junction with the Gran Vía, where the Cafetería Dolár now stands. Amid the panic one man found his hour. He was a retired matador named Diego Fortuny, who calmly sent his wife home to fetch his sword while he kept the bull in play with his coat. When she brought the sword he killed the bull with a single perfect *estocada* in the middle of the Alcalá.

I came upon such an ex-matador, but alas with no bull and the hour two o'clock on the icy morning of Christmas Day 1956 (just such a morning as that on which a chivalrous citizen took off his cloak of fine Bejar cloth and draped it over the frozen shoulders of Cybele, where the police found it at dawn), in the shape of an old man, penned by alcohol into a solitary dream-world of his own, fighting an imaginary bull in the middle of the frozen, deserted Gran Vía. He cited the bull from about thirty paces, Litri-fashion, waving away his *peones* like a cricket captain placing his field. (The characters with whom he peopled the street, bull and all, were as real as those with which the late Ruth Draper used to people her stage.) When, after a series of varied and elegant *muleta* passes with his coat, he went in over the horns to kill the absent bull, he fell flat on his face. He rolled over to avoid the horns, picked himself up and cited the bull once more, not a whit cast down.

Madrid was expanding steadily eastward along the Alcalá when Salamanca built a new ring further out, and in 1934 the present ring was built further out still at a spot called Las Ventas del Santo Espírito, just before the Alcalá crosses the gully of the Abronigal. El Monumental, as it is called, is the largest bullring in Spain and holds some twenty-three thousand spectators (or less than half the number which could see the fights from the balconies of the Plaza Mayor).

There are *corridas* every Sunday afternoon in the season and generally on Thursdays also, starting between four and seven according to the time of sundown. The season opens about the beginning of March with *novilladas* and the first proper *corrida* at Easter. Depending on the weather, it closes about the end of October. If you are in Madrid just outside these limits you can often in November or February see a charity fight to which the leading matadors give their services and the breeders their bulls free. You are not very likely to see any human blood shed, as the bulls' horns are allowed to be 'shaved' for these *beneficiencias*, and you miss the pageantry, as everyone wears not their 'suit of lights' but the ordinary Andalusian 'country costume'. On the other hand, you can be pretty sure of seeing half a dozen of the best bullfighters in Spain.

The best way to get tickets for the bulls is to put your hotel porter or buttons on to the job. The alternatives are to queue up at the official *taquilla* or booking office in the Calle Victoria or to go yourself to one of the *revendedores* or ticket brokers, such as Golidia in the Gran Vía. You can also take a chance of getting a ticket at the last moment at Las Ventas itself from the office outside the entrance to the ring. Sometimes the sign '*No Hay*' is hung up. This does not mean 'Please do not Feed the Animals' but 'House Full', and then your last and expensive resort is one of the ticket hustlers who hang around outside the ring and in the car park. Sometimes even they have all sold out and gone home.

The best and most expensive *tendidos* or sections in the Monumental are Numbers 9 and 10 in the shade under the President's box, where most of the action takes place and such distinguished visitors as 'resting' film stars and matadors sit in the *barreras*. (At every fight half a dozen retired *espadas* such as Vicente Pastor can be seen sitting in a row at the back of the President's box.) Another highly rated *tendido* is Number 8, where the *toreros* leave their capes. To take out an *abono* or subscription for the whole series of fights at San Isidro, as I have before now done, is quite an expensive business, but you can save a good deal of money by taking seats in the sun—in Tendido 6, for example; it is seldom inconveniently hot by the middle of May and the bullring is one of the few public places in Madrid where one may take off one's coat and sit in one's shirtsleeves. Moreover, the public in the sun is much better company, although one has to understand Spanish to understand their salty comments and all the barracking.

Madrid is the capital of the bullfighter's art and the Mecca of taurophiles from all over the world. There is no certainty on this earth of seeing a good fight but the best chance is in Madrid, where the public is the most discriminating and critical in the world. 'I am not severe; I am only just,' said Don Restituto, my tough, leathery-faced neighbour in Tendido 6 every afternoon for ten days one San Isidro, when I accused him of undue severity towards the *toreros*. Ears, tails and even hooves are awarded wholesale as trophies at provincial rings, but in Las Ventas no tails are ever given and even ears are hard to earn. Every successful Spanish *novillero* who wants to become a full-fledged *matador de toros* has to 'take his doctorate' or *alternativa*, or have it confirmed, in Madrid. (It rather corresponds to a barrister taking silk.) He is fully conscious of the publicity a good fight in Madrid will bring him. Nobody pays much attention to a fulsome paragraph from some provincial town but a *corrida* in Madrid may rate a couple of columns from an incorruptible critic in a national newspaper which will be read all over the country. Perhaps the best chance of a good fight is to see from the *carteles* or programmes what breeder is supplying the bulls. Some ranches generally produce good brave bulls and others seldom. Remember that the bull is the star and not the bullfighter, with the public making up the third in the emotional triangle. That is why the intense awareness of the expert public of Madrid stimulates the art and valour of a good matador.

To find out about the breed of bulls you must ask an *aficionado*. Indeed, the only way to learn about bulls is to talk bulls with the fans, to listen to their discussions and arguments, and to go to fights with a knowledgeable friend. If you have none such, invite a waiter or barman to come with you. He will be delighted to instruct you for the price of his ticket and he can generally manage to get a Sunday afternoon off. If he cannot, the night porter can.

Do not forget to take a clean white handkerchief to wave for an ear, but be very chary of waving it, as half your neighbours, Madrileños and therefore purists, will probably be against it and after all it is for them to uphold the austere tradition of the Madrid ring and not for the tourists to lower it. 'I never wave for an ear; if he gets it his price goes up and I have to pay more for my seat next time,' explained my neighbour, Don Restituto.

A *tarde de toros* is always an exception to all rules. It is a valid excuse if a policeman runs you in for speeding, and your taxi driver will ask you as his right for an extra five pesetas on the fare *'para los toros'*. If you are feeling rich, do not pay him at the time but tell him to wait and meet you at the end to take you home, as the public transport on a *tarde de toros* is to be avoided if at all possible. *Para los toros* is the phrase. The knowing talk of the fight and ring as 'the bulls' just as they talk of pelota as *'frontón'*. Thus friends will make an appointment to meet after *los toros* at, say, Bar Number 9 *en los toros*. 'Drink such and such *en los toros*', urge the liquor advertisements. But the real gaffe which brands the tenderfoot is to talk of a 'toreador', which is an obsolete word for the aristocratic mounted bullfighter abolished by Philip V two and a half centuries ago. Every bullfighter is a *torero* and the gladiators themselves are further called *matadores* or *espadas*, 'killers' or 'swords'.

One should always go in plenty of time to the bulls to

drink in the buzz and the excitement of the crowd and
the atmosphere which is like nothing else in the world,
to savour the smell of cattle and horses, to swallow the
ritual *copita* at the bar, to light the ritual cigar, to hire a
cushion for two pesetas and to find your seat. This last
in itself takes time and you give a peseta to the attendant
who does it for you. Remember that it is a difficult
afternoon to get a taxi; there is always a jam getting into
the ring; the fight starts on the dot; and if you are late
you will not be able to get in until the second bull and
then with only a lot of shoving and sweating and swear-
ing, publicity and embarrassment.

Once at least, it is worth while arriving three-quarters
of an hour early to visit the Taurine Museum, to which
many signs in the circular lobby all point. It contains
posters, portraits and historic relics in glass cases. In one
of them, the actual life blood of the legendary Manolete
still stains the *traje de luces* which he was wearing on that
last lethal afternoon at Linares.

CHAPTER NINE

The Prado

Southward from the Plaza de Cibeles runs the aptly named Salón de Prado, for during the last century it was almost literally the drawing room of Madrid. In the late eighteenth century the fashionable promenade of the capital was the Paseo de la Florida down by the river; then the Prado de Atocha, which was for many centuries an actual 'meadow' like the Roman Prati, praised by Lope de Vega and Quevedo and the scene of *verbenas* since Moorish times, was laid out and planted by Charles III. It was the great centre of elegant and literary Madrid in the Romantic period with carriage-folk and foot-folk making the *paseo* every evening between half past seven and ten. All the Romantic writers were on view, Espronceda, Zorrilla, Mesonero Romanos and the Duke of Rivas, and at their head strolled the exquisite figure of the Byronic poet, Mariano de Larra, who called himself Figaro, immaculate in blue frock coat, white trousers and stovepipe hat. The Palaces of the Dukes of Sesto, on the corner of the Alcalá where the Bank of Spain now is, of Villahermosa, still standing on the corner of the Plaza de Cortes, and, facing it, of Medinaceli on the Palace Hotel site, set the seal upon its dignity.

In 1775 Charles III's architect, Villanueva, built him a

neo-classical Museum of Natural History and Sciences a little lower down in the Paseo del Prado. It was originally a sort of annexe to the Botanical Gardens which the King had laid out in 1774, sending missions to different countries and ordering all his viceroys and governors to send him specimens of their local trees and plants. Charles III's order that medicinal herbs should be distributed free to the poor has never been rescinded and every morning between eleven and twelve o'clock people still come to the gate for their rue, sage, marjoram and other herbs. 'How many?' I asked the gatekeeper. He shrugged his shoulders. 'Sometimes a dozen and sometimes none,' he answered. Otherwise few people visit the garden despite its tree-shaded benches, fountains and statues, and it is a very peaceful, slightly melancholy, green oasis in the centre of Madrid.

In 1819 at the suggestion, it is said, of his Portuguese Queen, Ferdinand VII converted the museum into a picture gallery, installing there three hundred and eleven Spanish pictures from the royal collections. In 1840 Isabel II assembled here most of the important pictures from the various royal palaces, already concentrated in the Palacio de Oriente, and also from the many convents destroyed and secularised by Mendizábal. Velázquez' *Crucifixion* came from San Placido, for which it had been originally commissioned. The great Fra Angelico *Annunciation* was rescued from oblivion in the clausura of the Convent of the Descalzas Reales by Isabel II's husband, King Francisco de Asís, and the painter Madrazo, who gave the nuns in exchange a nice new modern picture—by Madrazo. As a result of all this, the Prado rapidly became one of the richest collections in Europe. In 1866 the

French critic, Louis Vierdet, pronounced it to be *the* richest.

The Prado now contains, in round figures, some eight hundred odd Spanish pictures, seven hundred Flemish, four hundred Italian, two hundred French, one hundred and fifty Dutch and fifty German. About half are actually on show. The wealth of the gallery is shown by the fact that it boasts no fewer than one hundred and fifteen Goyas, fifty Velázquez', fifty Riberas, thirty-nine Murillos, thirty-two El Grecos and twenty Zurbaráns; thirty-six Titians, twenty-eight Luca Giordanos, twenty-six Tintorettos, fifteen Veroneses and eight Raphaels; eighty-three Rubens, forty Jan Breughels, thirty-nine Teniers, thirty-three Van Dycks and fifteen Antonio Mors; twelve Poussins and ten Claudes; fourteen Dürers. Fourteen pictures are shown by all the English painters put together in a small round basement room which leads down from the buffet. There are two Spanish landscapes by Roberts and the others are nearly all portraits by the great English portrait painters. There is nothing by the great landscape painters such as Constable or Richard Wilson.

It is always interesting to know how a collection came together and why some schools are well represented while others are neglected. Thus the preponderance of Flemish over Dutch pictures in the Prado is largely due to the fact that Flanders was a part of the Spanish dominions, while Holland was a foreign and, for most of the time, an enemy country. Although Isabel la Católica was a patron of Flemish painting the nucleus of the royal collection was really formed by Charles V who, as heir to the Dukes of Burgundy, had inherited many Flemish and Burgundian works and to whom Pope Paul III used to send ancient sculpture from Rome. The sixteenth-century monarchs of Spain were themselves Flemings and they showed a great partiality for Flemish art. They also favoured the Venetians, and the Prado contains the best collection of that school outside Venice itself. Charles V had known Titian in Italy and commissioned many pictures from him, as did Philip II and Philip III from Tintoretto and Paolo Veronese.

Philip IV was a munificent patron of Rubens and gave him many commissions. He sent his Court Painter Velázquez to Italy to purchase works of art, of which some three hundred are now in the Prado. He also bought extensively at the auction of Charles I of England's collection when the Commonwealth sold it after his execution and 'at the tragic death of Charles, the care and labour of so many men fell to the ground in a day', as Velázquez wrote sadly.

Among the treasures now in the Prado of which England was robbed by her self-appointed Protector are Mantegna's *Dormition of the Virgin*, which the Spaniard Eugenio D'Ors said he would make a bee-line for if the Prado caught fire and he could only save one picture, Dürer's *Self-Portrait*, the Raphael *Holy Family* which Philip IV called *La Perla* because he considered it 'the pearl' of his collection, Andrea del Sarto's portrait of his naughty wife Lucrezia, Correggio's *Noli me Tangere*, three of the best Titians, including the *Reclining Venus*, Veronese's *Sacrifice of Abraham* and Tintoretto's lovely *Washing of the Feet*. It is small revenge that Van Eyck's *Arnolfini Family* in the National Gallery was for centuries in the Spanish Royal Collection until it was mysteriously 'liberated' during the Peninsular War.

The Frenchman Philip V added contemporary French paintings by Poussin, Claude and Watteau. His wife, Elizabeth Farnese, was a great admirer of Murillo and through Cardinal Acquaviva in Rome she also bought the collection of Queen Christina of Sweden, whence came most of the classical sculpture. The Lady of Elche arrived in the Prado as a result of a long peregrination which took her to the Louvre in Paris and to the Archaeological Museum in the Calle de Serrano.

The Prado is the only place in the world where Spanish painting can be properly studied and properly appreciated (though for Zurbarán and Murillo one has to go to Seville and Cádiz also, and for El Greco to Toledo). There is no need in this book to dwell upon the great Spanish masters, for every visitor will go to the six Goya rooms on the ground floor half-left of the main entrance. He will notice for himself the amazing differences in style and mood between the light, gay cartoons of the painter's youth (so much better than the actual tapestries at La Granja which were made from them), the bitter, satirical royal portraits of his middle period and the tortured fantasies in blacks and greys and browns, the so-called 'black pictures' which he painted for his own amusement (if one can use such an incongruous word) on the walls of the house on the bank of the Manzanares where he lived out his deaf and embittered old age.

He will notice also the differences in style between the official commissions of these painters and the pictures they made to please themselves, such as Goya's *Milkmaid of Bordeaux* and the very modern picture of the little dog in Room LI., Zurbarán's *Bodegón* and Velázquez's *Villa Medici*, which looks like an early Corot. On the first floor he will make his way to the magnificent rooms full of Velázquez, Zurbarán and Murillo—and Goya again. It is very easy (but most important not) to miss Velázquez's *Las Meninas*, which is all by itself in a sort of private ward. Stand by the painting and look in the mirror which has been fixed up (an ordinary looking-glass, believe it or not) to see this masterpiece in stereoscopic effect.

Once he has found them, the visitor has no need of a guide to the great Spaniards except his own eyes. Nevertheless, there are still a few gems in the Prado which, like *Las Meninas*, he might easily miss, especially if he is pressed for time. At the far end of the ground floor, on the right through the Rubens gallery, is the little South Rotunda, where he will find the lovely Lady of Elche, one of the finest pieces of antique sculpture in the world. It was discovered in the last century at Elche, the palm-embowered oasis near Alicante. While its origin is not precisely known, it is considered by many experts to be Iberian work of about 400 B.C., or shortly before the coming of the Carthaginians; others again believe it to be Greek.

Upstairs among the rich collection of Venetians are two of the finest pictures Tintoretto ever painted, the *Death of Holophernes* and the daring *Washing of the Feet*—the former with lighted figures standing out against a dark background, and the latter with a light foreground, the main theme and figures dark, and then again a luminous background of silver and blue stretching away in a long architectural perspective into the far distance. In one of the side galleries, is Mantegna's exquisite little *Dormition of the Virgin*, which backs on to a most extraordinary 'horror-comic-strip' by Botticelli, *The Story of Nastagio*

Degli Onesti (taken from the Decameron), and the great Fra Angelico *Annunciation*. In another side gallery is Hieronymous Bosch's masterpiece, *The Garden of Delights*. All these well repay a little search, when you have done with El Greco, Velázquez and Goya.

The Museum Quarter

Besides the Prado and the Museum of Plaster Casts, the Greek Quarter houses a number of small museums.

The Museum of Decorative Arts in the Calle de Montalbán houses a good collection of ceramics, Cordoba leather, glass, Neapolitan cribs and examples of domestic and ecclesiastical interiors.

The Military Museum, which illustrates the development of the Spanish Army, contains fifteenth-century artillery, uniforms, flags, weapons, trophies, models of fortresses, the war flags of Charles V and Cortes, and the campaign tent of Ferdinand and Isabella. One of the latest relics is the daily newsheet mimeographed in the Alcázar at Toledo during the siege of 1936.

The Marine Museum in the Ministry of Marines in the Calle de Montalbán performs the same function for the Navy. It houses over a hundred model ships, especially of the eighteenth century, fifteen thousand maps, plans and charts, and a hundred thousand documents dating between 1134 and 1794. To the layman the most interesting things are a very fine world map painted on an ox-hide by Juan de Costa of the year A.D. 1500, the first map to include the New World, sketches of Trafalgar and models of galleons; one of these latter shows a net spread to protect the crew from falling missiles and at the same

ALVAREZ ORTEGA

Plaza de la Academia

time to entangle boarders, as birdcatchers trap the feet of quail. The existence of this device was previously unknown to the learned Professor of Naval History whom I took to visit the Museum.

The Lottery

Just up the street from the Ministry of Marine is the headquarters of the Lottery Administration. To ask whether football is ousting bullfighting is rather like asking whether it is ousting cricket in England, for watching the one is a winter pastime and watching the other a summer one. Certainly the football fever in the winter is greater than the bull fever in the summer. The crowds which go to the big football matches fill giant stadia many times the size of the largest bullrings—but, of course, the tickets are a good deal cheaper. The Madrid bullring holds twenty-three thousand people while the football stadium seats five times as many. New bullrings, however, are always being built and opened all over Spain. The great fights, such as San Isidro, are always crammed, although 'westernised' Spaniards scornfully claim that bullfights exist for the tourists, not for them. More than that one cannot say.

Although Spaniards fill in their weekly football pools as Englishmen do, the real equivalent of our football pools is the National Lottery, imported from Italy two hundred years ago by Charles III's minister, the Marquis of Squillace (known to the Spaniards as Esquilace), who accompanied him when he exchanged the throne of Naples for that of Spain on the death of his brother,

Ferdinand VI. The original lottery consisted of only ninety numbers and five prizes, but in 1812 the Cortes Constituyentes of Cádiz reformed it, enlarged it and gave it its present name of the *Lotería Nacional*. The object of the operation, then as now, is not just to provide everyone with a bit of innocent fun, but to raise revenue for the State as painlessly as possible; it is, in fact, a classic example of voluntary taxation.

The lottery is drawn every ten days, generally on the 5th, 15th and 25th of each month. The price varies but ranges from ten pesetas, through fifteen, twenty-five, fifty, one hundred and two hundred, up to four hundred for the great Christmas charity draw—*El Sorteo de Navidad*. These prices are for tenths of a ticket, such as are usually sold by the ticket-pedlars, for only a very hardy gambler would think of buying a whole ticket. If, for example, any non-fictional character wanted to stake the four thousand pesetas which is the price of a whole ticket for the Christmas lottery, thus giving himself a theoretical but quite astronomical chance of 'touching' fifteen million pesetas if he won *El Gordo*, 'The Fat One', he would almost certainly buy ten separate *décimos* and thus decuple his chances of winning at least something. Often, however, whole tickets are bought and parcelled out in innumerable small portions by a street, a factory or an office, and if it wins the whole neighbourhood shares in the rejoicing and half of it sees its photograph in the national newspapers.

This is the way it works. The more expensive lottery generally takes place at the beginning of the month, when monthly-salary-earners are supposed to be flush with cash, and the ten-peseta draws on the 25th, when they have spent their pay. The end-of-the-month lottery distributes nearly four million pesetas in prize money, and the cheapest ticket you can buy is a *décimo* for ten pesetas (or rather eleven, for you give one as a tip to the seller and more, proportionally, for the more expensive draws). There are first, second and third prizes of forty thousand, twenty thousand and ten thousand pesetas, eight of six hundred, and a thousand, six hundred and fifty nine prizes of one hundred if your two final digits are the same as the two final digits of the first prizewinner; and two hundred and ninety-seven of one hundred for the remaining numbers of the same century as one of the first three prizewinners; six prizes of six hundred, three hundred and one hundred for the numbers next to the three big prizewinners; and no fewer than five thousand five hundred and ninety-nine ten-peseta prizes for the final numbers identical with the final number of the first prizewinner. All these prizes are listed on the backs of the tickets.

The prizes for the more expensive draws are, of course, proportionate to the price of the tickets, so that the great Christmas Lottery can net you a million and a half pesetas for an outlay of four hundred. It comes in nine separate series, each of sixty thousand tickets; each series distributes a complete set of prizes worth eighty-two million, nine hundred and eight thousand pesetas. The whole lottery (which is usually sold out), disposes of a total sum of one thousand and eighty million pesetas, of which 69·09% is distributed in prize money and 31·91% goes to the Spanish Treasury and for running expenses. So, all in all, it is pretty big business.

To find out if you have won you read the papers on the

morning after (not on the evening of) the draw, ask any
lottery-ticket seller for the list, which he should carry
on him, or go and look at it outside one of the lottery-
offices. (There are several in the Gran Vía and the Alcalá.)
To get paid out on your wins you go to the lottery-office
whose address is stamped on the back of your ticket.

Flamenco

Better a grave and a measured fandango
Than trying to dance some damfool tango.

Next to the bulls, the most characteristically Spanish
entertainment is the combination of song and dance
known by the generic name of flamenco. Indeed, the
two are more closely linked than might be at first
supposed. No one who has seen a bullfight and then goes
on to watch flamenco can fail to notice how closely the
dance movements parallel the motions of playing a bull—
what the late Roy Campbell, translating the untranslatable word *torear*, called torrying.

Although no proof is ever likely to be forthcoming, it
seems more than likely that both arts were introduced
into Spain by the Minoans, or at least by the Greeks,
through the southern ports (old Phoenician colonies
both) of Cádiz and Huelva, which was the Greek Tar-
tessos and the Hebrew Tarshish; Cretan vases show men
torrying with bulls, and the Labyrinth of Minos was
probably a bullring. Similarly, Greek and Cretan vases
show women dancing in a very similar manner to the
flamenco dancers of today.

'*Jocosae Gades*', or 'gay Cádiz', exported dancers as lewd as they were agile, the *improbae Gaditanae* whom the Early Fathers compared to Salome, all over the Roman Empire until they were forbidden by Theodosius.

About the derivation of the word flamenco nothing is sure except that it does not mean what it says—'Flemish'. The *flamencos* or Flemings came to Spain in the train of Charles V, who was born Charles of Ghent, but they had little connection with these exotic Oriental dances. Apart from the institution of the kermesse and a tapestry factory, they left only a few not very complimentary sayings, such as '*muy flamenco*' for rowdy and boisterous behaviour. One theory is that flamenco in the terpsichorean sense is derived from the Arabic *fellah-menkus*, the 'exiled peasants' from a civil war in North Africa who were granted lands in Spain, but certainly, despite obvious Arab and gipsy influence, the dance existed a thousand years and perhaps two before the Moors came to Spain.

And where to see Spanish dancing in Madrid? There are occasional flamenco turns in the ordinary night-club (euphemistically known as *salas de fiestas*); there are one or two smart restaurant night-clubs which specialise in good flamenco such as El Corral de la Morería and El Duende. If you want a private show, you can lay on a *cuadro de flamenco* for a very moderate price at various bars such as the Villa Rosa in the Plaza de Santa Ana which have private rooms for the purpose, but these parties are best arranged in advance through some local friend. Or again there is La Zambra at 7 Calle de Ruiz de Alarcón just around the corner from the Ritz Hotel in the Barrio Griego.

The Zambra was originally started and sponsored,

although never run, by the Dirección General de Turismo
to prevent tourists who wanted to see flamenco from
being fleeced in the gipsy joints as they once used to be.
It is itself far from cheap; there is no entrance fee, but the
price of the first consummation (the later drinks are
cheaper) is such that you might as well order whisky,
since it costs the same as coffee. Under the direction of
the expert Don Carlos Boyer, the Zambra is dedicated
to the old 'pure' or classical *cante jondo*, of which the so-
called *cante flamenco* is a popularised version. The stage
reproduces a typical Andalucian *café cantante* of sixty
years ago, and the whole evening is one to remember, for
the standard of singing and dancing is perhaps the highest
in all Spain.

The Archaeological Museum

On the other side of the Alcalá is the large building which
houses the National Library with its entrance on the
Paseo de los Recoletos, and the Archaeological Museum,
the Museum of Modern Art and the Museum of America,
all of which one enters from the Calle de Serrano. The
titles of all three museums are somewhat misleading, it
may be said.

The Archaeological Museum not only includes exhibits
of ancient material but carries some of the minor arts
right on up to the eighteenth century. Of the classical
finds one of the most interesting objects to me was an
Ibero-Roman bronze bull from Azaita near Teruel with
its *morrillo* or tossing muscle raised exactly as it is in
fighting bulls today; *bos taurus ibericus* can hardly have

changed since the days when it roamed wild over the great empty uplands of Castile. The works of the Iberians, Phoenicians, Carthaginians, Greeks, Romans and Visigoths are represented in turn, the last named including the silver votive crowns studded with gems and other jewellery recently found near Toledo. They are comparable with the contemporary Lombard work to be seen in Monza and Brescia. Then come examples of mediaeval Christian and Moslem art. There are a number of English alabasters of the fourteenth and fifteenth centuries. (In the little cathedral of Sigüenza, remote and isolated on the Castilian prairies, I came by chance upon a fine alabaster triptych of the Nottingham School.) Particularly impressive are the massive embroidered hangings of the Conde-Duque de Olivares, whom Velázquez painted, and some beautiful Hispano-Mauresque pottery.

The Museum of Modern Art

The Museum of Modern Art is remarkable rather for what it lacks than for what it contains. There are roomfuls of enormous and pretty deplorable nineteenth-century historical paintings and also some works by meritorious early twentieth-century painters such as Zuloaga, Sorolla and Solano. Except for one curious early Picasso which one might almost take for a Beardsley, modern paintings are practically unrepresented. One can perhaps understand a conservative committee regarding Salvador Dalí with some suspicion, even though he is by far the most famous painter now living in Spain, but one looks in

vain for the more conventional masters such as José María
Sert and Beltrán-Masses. Joan Miró is not here and even
the Madrileño Juan Gris, who has six paintings in the
Tate Gallery, is without a single authenticated one in
his own native city, where he started his career as a
young man drawing for the weekly *Blanco Y Negro*.
The Museum of Modern Art is in fact a museum of
nineteenth- and early twentieth-century painting, and
not even complete at that.

This criticism is hardly invalidated by the recently
founded little Museum of Contemporary Art which,
like its larger neighbour, contains none of these painters
except two small paintings of Gris, both queried, and one
very early and purely conventional Dalí of 1925.

Americana

The museum in all Madrid most easy to miss is the
Museum of America, for it is not in most of the guide-
books nor even in the very comprehensive plan at the
entrance to the Archaeological Museum, on the first floor
of which it is temporarily housed, pending the comple-
tion of its new home in University City.

Remember that in Spain an *americano* is a Latin American and an American in Spanish is a *norteamericano*, and
you will realise why there is nothing in the Museum of
America which comes from north of the Rio Grande
except a solitary painted buffalo-hide.

The nucleus of the collection was formed by some
'curiosities' presented to the Museum of National
Sciences when it occupied the Prado, in the shape of

some Maya carvings from the Palenque excavations of 1785 and some Peruvian ceramics sent home in 1788.

This must be one of the finest collections of pre-Colombian art in the world, for to celebrate the fourth centenary of the Discoverer in 1892 the Government of Colombia presented Queen Maria Cristina with the rich Quimbaya treasure of gold ornaments, and the Peruvian Government with a superb collection of pottery. I have seldom seen such an exciting exhibition as these Chimú and proto-Chimú pots; some are beautiful, some humorous, some sinister but, whatever exactly 'significant form' may be, one recognises it to the highest degree in all of them.

Other treasures of the Museum include the amazing Aztec cloaks, hats and even pictures and carpets confected with the bright feathers of tropical birds, and fascinating necklaces made of the iridescent green shards of Mexican beetles. Two Maya codices, out of only four known examples; two very rare sets of 'colonial' pictures painted on wood and inlaid with mother-of-pearl; dozens of wax figures of Mexican types of the early nineteenth century; such are some of the rarities of this secret treasure house.

The Ball Game

In the Calle de Villanueva beside the Archaeological Museum is the Recoletos restaurant where you can dine and dance in the intervals of watching the ball game in the adjoining frontón. The Frontón de los Recoletos is the most fashionable *frontón* or pelota court in Madrid.

(The most central one, the Frontón Madrid, is in the Calle del Doctor Cortezo.) This is a Basque game which goes under various names; in English it is usually known as pelota, which means simply 'ball'; the Basque for it is *jai alai*; the Madrileños call it *frontón* from the court it is played in.

The court is the size of a small country cathedral. There are seats along one side of it, separated from the court itself by stout wire netting. The other side and the ends are solid. The seats rise in three tiers like the stalls, dress circle and upper circle of a theatre. Below, where the orchestra would be in a theatre, a row of bookmakers, all in short black coats like stockbroker's clerks, shout the latest odds.

The game is practically a monopoly of Basque professionals, and is played in teams of two-a-side, who are distinguished from each other by blue and red sashes. Handicapping is done by advancing the service line. There are two varieties of *frontón*; one is played with a small flat bat and the other with a wicker attachment strapped to the hand and resembling the long curved digging claw of an ant-eater, which can equally well hit or catch the ball. Either way it is one of the fastest games in the world and the ball travels with such force and speed that it is often impossible to see it at all.

High on the wall opposite the public is a scoreboard marking up the points in red and blue respectively, and the odds change all the time according to the score. Betting is high. The stake unit at the Frontón de los Recoletos is eighty duros or four hundred pesetas. A call of 'Twenty!' means that the odds are eighty duros to twenty, or 'Thirty!', eighty to thirty—and so forth as the game progresses. The big betting men sit mostly in the *palcos*, the front rows of the dress circle; the bookies call the odds and the punters bet on red by putting a hand to their cheek or on blue by putting a hand to their sleeves. The bookie throws up a betting slip stuffed into a sort of scooped out tennis ball. The backer pulls out the slip, puts the money into the ball and throws it back to the bookie. In addition to an eye for winners, the chief requisite for the successful punter at *frontón* seems to be an ability to catch and throw a tennis ball—which would disqualify me right away.

Another popular indoor ball game in Madrid is *bolera*, which the English call skittles and the Americans call bowling. There are a good many bowling alleys in Madrid. Some of the handiest for anyone who wants to watch the sport are the Boliches at Calle de Fernando El Santo 24 near the British Embassy; La Bolería Carlos III at Calle de Goya 5, and the Bilbao at Calle de Fuencarral 118. These *bolerías* open at midday and remain open serving drinks and light meals—this is worth remembering when everything else is shut—until three in the morning.

Little Weights

Just to the north of the Palace of the Museums is the old Mint where for many years Spanish coins have been minted. Now a new Mint is being built elsewhere and the site is to be turned into an open space flanked by two exhibition buildings. The peseta or 'little weight' was invented on October 19th, 1868, when the decimal coinage was introduced into Spain. It was established as the basic unit of the new currency, but the coin which really caught the imagination of the public was 'the hard one', the *duro* or five-peseta piece, a magnificent silver coin like a British crown piece or a Mexican dollar. The lower classes, especially in the country, have not entirely absorbed the new coinage, which after all has only been in force for less than a century. Since the disappearance of the old copper coinage it is less common to hear people in the capital talk to a foreigner of a *real*, which is twenty-five centimos, a *perra gorda* or 'fat bitch', which is ten centimos, and a *perra chica* or 'little bitch', which is five centimos; they took their names from the lion on the obverse of the coin. In the country one is often quoted such a cryptic price as *siete chicas*, which is to be interpreted as thirty-five centimos.

When I first came to Spain thirty years ago nobody talked of centimos; all small prices were in *chicas* and *reales*. Even though these terms are going out in Madrid, the people still reckon not in pesetas but in *duros*. Thus for five hundred pesetas they say *cien duros*. You will see them mentally dividing by five and converting pesetas into *duros*. They will quote prices in *duros* and often, just to make it more confusing, leave out the word *duros*, mentioning only the figure. So then it is you who have to adjust the price and do some mental arithmetic to reach pesetas.

Until 1931 these *duros* were common currency. They were the last genuine coins left anywhere in Europe since the Albanian gold napoleons were rounded up by the Italians in 1927. After 1931 there were still handsome, but far from silver, *duros* in circulation until they also were withdrawn in 1958 and replaced first by notes and then by maddening, confusing little coins which are practically indistinguishable from ten-centimo pieces. It is a pity, for these handsome silver cartwheels were much more in keeping with the Spanish character and scene than bits of paper. They were devilish hard on the trouser pockets, but one cannot expect to handle and jingle such beautiful objects without corresponding disadvantages.

Be very careful not to lose cheques, as Spanish cheques are all made out 'to bearer' and can be cashed by anybody who endorses them. Most people change their money and travellers' cheques at a bank, but the big hotels will give a worse exchange of no more than about a peseta in the pound and will do a job for you in three minutes which will take you anything up to half an hour in a bank. Moreover, they will change your money when the banks are shut or when you have left your passport at home. You must, of course, look passably honest and respectable—yet another of the hundred and one reasons for not walking about in Madrid in a khaki shirt and shorts.

Recoletos

The Paseo de los Recoletos has been officially rechristened the Avenida de Calvo Sotelo after the proto-martyr of the 'Crusade', who was murdered in 1936. (The symbolical martyr is José Antonio Primo de Rivera, which is why you see the words 'José Antonio' stencilled on the façades of the churches.) It is, however, always known in the demotic by its old name of Recoletos. Similarly the Gran Vía is officially called the Avenida de José Antonio, but a taxi-driver once lectured me severely

for a quarter of an hour for directing him to 'José
Antonio'. 'Its proper name is the Gran Vía,' he snorted,
'and we Madrileños all call it the Gran Vía.'

Bars

Twenty years of the nagging (even if not entirely un-
provoked) anti-British propaganda in the Spanish press
which preceded Spain's long overdue re-admission to the
comity of nations have had little effect on the average
Spaniard, who seems as friendly and courteous as he ever
was, nor oddly enough on the number of English (as
distinct from American) names to be seen about Madrid.

One of the biggest department shops in Madrid is called
El Corte Inglés, and the smart place to go for baby-linen
and layettes is El Bebé Inglés. The fashionable cloak-
maker in the Calle de la Cruz is called El Escudo Inglés.
A shoe shop in the Calle de Sevilla is called Oxford and
there is a dress shop in the Calle de las Infantas called
Rosa Tudor or Tudor Rose. Ana Bolena, the name of
a smart beauty shop, is none other than our own Anne
Boleyn, a figure who has a peculiar and sinister place in
Spanish mythology as the beautiful witch who lured
Henry VIII away from Catherine of Aragon and so lost
England for the Faith. (Clearly any English woman who
could get a man away from a Spanish woman, with or
without the aid of the Devil, must be worthy to give her
name to a beauty shop.) The Victoria Cruz Bar on the
corner of the Calle de Victoria and the Calle de la Cruz
probably has no connection with the Victoria Cross, but
one wonders how the Brunswick Billiard Saloon in the

Calle del Prado got its name—clearly a military one or the German Braunschweig would not have come in its English form. Were one sufficiently interested to write to the War Office, one would probably discover that the Black Brunswickers entered Madrid with Wellington in 1812. But sometimes it is more agreeable to guess than to play the historian. Anyhow, this German word which has come thus anglicised to Spain may be taken as a fair revenge for the 'Scottish' which has entered Spanish as a popular dance called *chotís* by way of the German *Schottische*.

Above all, there is the Balmoral on the right or Serrano side where the Paseo de los Recoletos becomes the Paseo de la Castellana. It is founded and owned by Señor Feliú, the former head barman of the Palace Hotel, and is perhaps the most fashionable bar in Madrid at the moment. It strives to reproduce the atmosphere of Scotland at Calle de Hermosilla 10. You will never find the Balmoral if you tell the taxi-driver to drive to the Balmoral with the accent on the o. He has never heard of it. It is pronounced like a moral French dance—Bal m'ral. (Why has nobody ever started up a night spot called *Le Bal Immoral*?) The Balmoral is crammed every midday and every evening with the cream of Castellana and Salamanca society; though few foreigners seem to find their way there, it is dedicated mainly to the consumption of Scotch whisky, a drink which is practically *de rigueur*, at whatever financial sacrifice, for any Spaniard with a social position to lose or to keep up. From the look of it one would imagine that it must use up in a month the annual legal imports of that liquor into Spain.

Over the bar hang the triple emblems of the British

civilising mission, a golf club, a polo stick and a cricket bat. There are assorted stuffed grouse and a number of horned heads which were certainly never shot in Scotland unless they were poached in the Edinburgh Zoo. To find a capercailzie it is necessary to go to the Embassy Tea Room, nearby on the Castellana, but the Balmoral boasts two stuffed bustards, with arched necks, scornful eyes and fierce moustachios, and looking far haughtier than any Spanish grandee ever looked in his life. The climax of *écossaiserie*, however, is an enormous copy of the well-known whisky advertisement showing the kilted young chieftain interrupted in his solitary tippling by his alcoholic ancestors stepping out of their picture frames to steal their descendant's drink (unless it is only an attack of D.T.'s). It is surely the cruellest of all the stories the Scotch like to tell against themselves.

Another good place to drop in for a drink is Mansard's in the Alcalá, on the left just before you come to the Plaza de la Independencia. If you go in you will probably see a small, square septuagenarian, drifting from table to table. It is Monsieur Mansard, bar-owner, racehorse-owner, bloodstock-dealer, the last living pupil of the great Escoffier, and, with forty years of Madrid behind him, perhaps the most popular Frenchman in a city which shows its general opinion of its northern neighbours over a small door in the airport where they arrive, succinctly inscribed 'Caballeros—Hommes—Gentlemen'.

If you have an English paper under your arm, he will very likely ask to have a look at it and turn straight to the sporting page. 'Thank you. Just wanted to see what 'orses were runnin' at Wolver'ampton', he will explain as he returns it in some disorder. He started his career as a boy in the kitchens of the Duke of Westminster at Eaton Hall, went on to the Ritz in London and was brought to Spain by Escoffier when the Madrid Ritz was opened in 1910. He was for many years chef to the Duke of Medinaceli, probably the richest grandee in Spain, and was the first manager of Gaylord's Restaurant when it was opened in 1930 as the most fashionable in Madrid. Subsequently he started his own bar. He has made it rather like a London club with panelled walls and leather armchairs, and the barman can shake a good Dry Martini.

Mansard's is always crowded and almost entirely by Spaniards. It is not, like the Balmoral, a resort of noble-men and society ladies so much as of racing and betting men, attracted by M. Mansard's own interest in the turf. Often of an afternoon you will see long and earnest sessions of poker-dice at one of those round tables made with a raised rim, which are so inconvenient for writing at or taking tea off, but so handy for preventing the dice from rolling on to the floor.

These two, with the bar of the Palace Hotel, form the trinity of smart bars where the Madrileños go. (They are all respectable bars where you can ask your wife to meet you—though here and there the sharp-eyed will notice a couple of very demure and expensive cocottes.) They have their runners up such as Regny's, almost next door to the Balmoral, the Club 31 opposite Mansard's and the Castellana Hilton, which is frequented largely by Americans and is the meeting place for all the film people in town, who go there to pick up the latest gossip and to try and get jobs out of each other. It is a curiously con-structed bar and one feels rather like being inside a roll-top desk (just as to be in the Church of San Bernardo in Rome

F

feels like being inside a golf ball). The younger set of Spaniards frequents the bars and cafés in the Calle de Serrano or places like the Indiana in the Calle de los Recoletos where there is music. Recently a number of small, intimate bar-night-clubs have sprung up, many of them cashing in on the whisky-snobbery by giving themselves such names as Scotch 52, Whisky a Gogo, Whisky Jazz and Whisky Gin.

Anglicisms

On the left of the Paseo de la Castellana is the 'Embassy Quarter', so-called because it contains most of the diplomatic missions, for which reason it remained practically unbombed and a sort of city of refuge all through the Civil War. The British Embassy is at Calle Fernando el Santo 16 (telephone 23 28 10) with the entrance to the Consulate just around the corner in the Calle de Monte Esquinzo (telephone 24 65 20). The American Embassy and Consulate are located at Calle de Serrano 75 (telephone 36 36 00); the Canadian Embassy is in the Edificio España at Avenida de José Antonio 88 (telephone 47 54 00); the Irish Embassy is at Calle de Goya 53 (telephone 25 16 85); the Pakistan Embassy at Calle de Almagro 36 (telephone 57 20 07) and the Indian Embassy at Calle Alfonso XII 46 (telephone 39 02 52). The South African Legation is at Paseo de la Castellana 1 (telephone 23 49 31). Australia, New Zealand and Ceylon use the services of the British Embassy.

Not far from the Embassy at Calle de Almagro 5 is the British Institute, with an excellent library which it is possible to join for a small subscription. The British Embassy Church is at Calle de Hermosilla 43 on the corner of the Calle de Nuñez de Balboa in the Salamanca Quarter. If you are ill, ring up the British-American Hospital (it is on the edge of University City where the Calle de Isaac Peral becomes the Calle Limite) on number 34 67 00; if it is your car which requires treatment, try the Salamanca Garage at 41 Calle de Bretón de los Herreros on telephone number 34 20 21; it is the agent for a number of British makes of cars.

The Instituto Valencia de Don Juan

Just off the Paseo de la Castellana at Calle de Fortuny 9 is a private art institute which is interesting both for the contents of its museum, which is open free to the public, and for its close links with England. The founder, Don Guillermo de Osma, Count of Valencia de Don Juan, was an Oxford man and left £3,000 to found a bursary for an Oxford student to come to Madrid every year and study Spanish art. He also appointed the Vice-Chancellor of Oxford and the Keeper of Antiquities at the British Museum *ex-officio* members of the Board of Trustees of his Institute in Madrid. He amassed an interesting collection of jewellery from prehistoric to modern times (and a unique set of Spanish horse-brasses), but the chief reason for a visit is what is claimed to be the finest collection in the world of that Hispano-Mauresque pottery with the metallic glaze of which the secret is now apparently lost. The Hispano-Mauresque ceramics of this type now to be seen in the Victoria and Albert Museum were presented by Don Guillermo's widow.

The Museo Lázaro-Galdiano

A leading figure in the literary world of the 'nineties was a young Navarrese named Don José Lázaro-Galdiano, proprietor of a successful publishing firm called La España Moderna. A lifelong collector, he bought the first item in his museum, a medallion of Alfonso V, for two *duros* when he was a boy of fourteen. In his retirement he devoted his life and the fortune he had made out of publishing to the formation of one of the richest private art collections in Europe—a sort of Spanish Wallace Collection.

In 1908 he bought a property and built a three-storey house, surrounded by a garden complete with English gardeners, at 122 Calle de Serrano just beyond the American Embassy and the British Ambassador's residence. He called it the Parque Florido after his wife, an Argentine lady named Paula Florido. There among his treasures the white-bearded hermit lived for another thirty years hardly seeing a soul until he died in 1948 at the age of eighty-six and left his house and all that it contained to the Spanish State.

The richness and variety of the collection can be seen from the Artists' Catalogue whose seven hundred names run through the alphabet from Abadía to Zurbarán. The collection of Limoges enamels is one of the finest in Europe. There are, in addition, magnificent collections of Florentine Renaissance bronzes, mediaeval ivories (many of them English), mediaeval and antique jewellery and Byzantine carvings. The pictures include not only all the great Spanish painters, including a roomful of Goyas, but such foreign masters as Leonardo, Rembrandt and Dürer. There is a whole roomful of English pictures by Gainsborough, Romney, Hoppner, Lawrence, Richard Parkes Bonington and others. It feels strange to come upon Constable's *Old Mill* in sunny Madrid. There are more English pictures here than there are in the Prado and more than I can think of off-hand in any Continental gallery except perhaps the Pininski in Cracow. (In all Italy I can only recollect two, Lawrence's *George IV* in the Vatican Gallery and a Zoffany in Cortona.) In the room of miniatures (XXVI) just beyond the English room, look for the masterly little portrait of the Duchess of Châteauneuf, a symphony in white and several shades of green which, although conventionally accurate, gives at first the impression of an abstract geometrical design drawn with a pair of compasses.

CHAPTER TEN

The Castellana

Beyond the Museum the Calle de Serrano runs out into El Viso, one of the new, expensive, still not quite finished, quarters of Madrid, even now popularly known as *El Fin de Serrano*. It centres around the Hotel Commodore in the Plaza de la República Argentina, which seems to be still waiting for Madrid to grow out to it.

What is now the Paseo de la Castellana was a rubble-filled gully used as a rubbish dump until in the 1830's it was cleaned up and laid out as a Paseo by an energetic *alcalde* called the Marqués de Pontejos and succeeded the Prado as the chic promenade of the capital.

Called after the Fuente Castellana, whose water Cervantes praised as *extremadísima* for freshness and transparency, there were in about 1870 only two or three houses here, but the contemporary newspapers wrote that 'elegant society shows itself during the season in the traditional *paseo* of the Fuente Castellana and parades in luxurious carriages the extensive *alameda* between the Obelisk and the Recoletos gardens.' The Castellana became the most fashionable quarter of Madrid, but now the old Wimbledon-type houses with their private gardens are mostly turned into offices and further along rise new blocks such as the Castellana Hilton Hotel, a corner of the U.S.A. transplanted, prices and all, to

Madrid. Beyond the gigantic and for decades uncompleted new Ministries, the Castellana becomes the Avenida del Generalísimo, lined by towering blocks of flats, many of them seemingly abandoned when half built and others so thickly populated by American families as to be nicknamed 'Little Korea'. On the right is the suburb of Chamartín, where Napoleon had his headquarters and whence he dictated the surrender of Madrid in 1808, and the immense football ground, the Estadio Bernabéu, where a hundred and twenty thousand people can sit and watch the triumphs of Real Madrid.

Taxis and Transport

Long years of driving on the Continent have convinced me that, for once in a way, everybody is out of step except the English and that it is as natural for the average man to drive on the left of the road as it is for him to shave with his right hand. Be that as it may, motorists in Spain are supposed to keep to the right. Otherwise the rules of the road differ little from those in England, since common sense everywhere prescribes much the same methods of avoiding accidents. Nevertheless, there are a few which the motorist should memorise, if he does not wish to be fined—and the pedestrian also, for he too is subject to the discipline of the traffic police. He also, logically enough, is held responsible for trying to avoid accidents on the road.

One important thing for the motorist to remember in Madrid is that hooting is abolished and sounding his horn will render him liable to a fine. Parking is forbidden within five metres of a street corner or of a bus or tram stop. In a two-way street you park on the right; in a one-way street you park before even-numbered houses (i.e. those on the right going away from the Puerta del Sol or the left going towards it) on even days of the month, and before odd-numbered on uneven dates. If this system avoids the chaos of narrow London Streets with cars parked on both sides, it has the disadvantage that to work it you need to carry a calendar and preferably a compass as well. It also means that if you leave your car on the right side of the road in the evening it is on the wrong side by next morning.

When trams run in the centre of a two-way street, you pass on the right or inner side. When the street is one-way only for cars, you may pass on either side. You give way to vehicles coming in from your right unless you are covered by a green light, and also to fire engines and motor-ambulances even if you are. (The latter race about Madrid, blowing their sirens as they go, in enormous quantities.) The object of this rule is to avoid having to look both ways at every crossroad, but it is modified when there is a major road ahead. One of the most important signs for the motorist to recognise, therefore, is a circular blue disc bearing in white the legend *Ceda el Paso—Give Right of Way*. Fortunately the command is as easy to remember as it is vital—'Yield the Pass!'. The sign for a One-Way Street is a red disc with a white strip across it, and with good sight and experience one learns to distinguish it quite easily from the ubiquitous *Coca-Cola* signs.

Pedestrians are not allowed to cross the main streets except by a recognised crossing with traffic lights or a policeman. The green light stays on a perilously short time and you can launch yourself halfway across the road, only to be enveloped in a flood of traffic when it changes to red. The crowds pile up on either pavement and when the signals change the front ranks charge into the road towards each other (the lame and the halt with a pathetic panic-stricken gait like the spavined gallop of picadors' horses). Halfway across comes what the Spaniards call 'the moment of truth' and it requires but little imagination to see the two waves rise in the air in spume as they meet.

In England a middle-income man will run a car but will not run to cigars, whereas in Spain he will be able to smoke plenty of cigars but not to keep a car which is, in his country, a symbol of wealth like a cigar in England. There is a 130% duty on cars in Spain, not to mention a long and almost hopeless waiting list for licences. That is why, not counting the odd little bubble-cars and *biscuteros*, which not only sound but look like biscuit tins but are really 'bi-scooters' or double scooters, there are only a hundred thousand cars in Madrid, or a third of the number in Rome with much the same population. This makes driving here much easier, although visitors direct from England often find it frightening enough. A witty English lady of my acquaintance remarked that in Portugal an accident is a *desastre*, whereas in Spain it is acclaimed as a *suceso* and in Italy shrugged off as an *incidente*.

A green number plate means a provisional licence, with the proper number still unallotted. The common plate OP means the Ministry of Public Works or *Obras Públicas*, while PMM is the Ministerial Car Park, *Parque*

Mobíl Ministerial, which the cynical Madrileños interpret as '*Para Mi Mujer*'—'for my wife'. Like all Latins they enjoy these plays upon initials and they affect to believe that 'CD' or *Cuerpo Diplomático* stands for *Caras Duras*, and Vespa for *Vosotros Españoles Sereis Pronto Americanos*.

Before this digression we were in the Avenida del Generalísimo and from this frozen black river of asphalt which runs interminably between the sandhills on the one side and the high red cliff-dwellings of the Americans on the other we must return to the Plaza de Cibeles, now, with the eastward expansion of Madrid, practically its geographical centre, as the Puerta del Sol was in the old days. We can walk between the trees down the Castellana —but it is a long way; or plunge into the Metro—but none of the Sol-centred lines run down the Castellana; or climb on to a bus—as long as it is not in the rush hours. (A Madrid paper recently carried a cartoon of sardines being packed in a tin and protesting: 'What do you think we are? Human beings?') Perhaps after all the simplest way is to take a taxi.

Look carefully when picking yourself a taxi, for some of them bear the number 3 in a circle pasted on the windscreen. This means that they have no tip-up seats and are only allowed to take three passengers instead of the usual five. The old Seat taxis of Madrid made in Barcelona under licence from the Turin firm of Fiat are, for long-legged men, elaborate instruments of torture, for they have only a small door to creep in and out through, being as low in the roof as they are high off the ground. Leg-room is further reduced when they stop right up against a high kerb (and you are only allowed to get in and out on the pavement side). Often one can only clamber in on

hands and knees or alight by sitting on the floor and
easing oneself out. Sitting with knees doubled up one
still bumps one's head. Always choose one of the new
Seats or Austins if possible.

Free taxis can be recognised by the placard '*Libre*' in
front of the driver or can be picked out at night by a
green light on the roof. At normal times there are plenty
of taxis in Madrid. In fact, there are nearly six thousand
of them, or more than there are in the whole of London
and nearly three times as many as in Rome—both of them
cities, of course, with a much denser car population. But
the taxis tend to disappear from the streets in a tantalising
fashion just when one needs them most. Curious and
almost unique complaint though it may be, the trouble
is that they are too cheap. When it rains everybody hails
a taxi—people whose opposite numbers in London would
never dream of such an extravagance. Richer people, who
in England would probably have their own car, hire a
taxi and keep it for hours or, in wet weather, all day.
Especially on the afternoons of football matches and bull-
fights taxis vanish altogether, since patrons take them
out to the spectacle and keep them for the drive home
again. *La hora crítica*, as it is called, when it is almost
impossible to get a taxi, is from eight o'clock in the
evening onwards when everybody is leaving his office
and going home or out to a cocktail party. A secondary
peak of scarcity occurs about three o'clock in the afternoon when the taxi-drivers go home to have lunch.

Hippophiles who regret the old days of horse-cabs can
nevertheless warm to the taxis of Madrid, for before
General Primo de Rivera introduced the *peto* or shield
for bullring horses the Madrid cabhorses were the main

source of supply. Now that they no longer exist the *peto* can never be abolished. Apart from the fact that the old gory sights hold no attraction for the public (which, believe it or not, goes to see art and not blood) even the horse contractors, whose interest is to supply as many Rosinantes as possible for the padded, pompom-hatted Sancho Panzas to ride, admit that it would be quite impossible for lack of horses to return to the old days when maybe a dozen were killed in every fight. As a matter of record, a single bull in Tudela once killed seventeen horses.

The Cries of Madrid

Madrid once had the reputation of being not only the latest but the noisiest city in Europe. Until all hours of the morning trams screeched; cars drove continuously on their klaxons; exhausts roared; pedlars of all kinds shouted their wares. Now all is changed. A decree of 1956 abolished hooting, open exhausts and loud radios. Only the loudspeaker vans seem still to defy the edict, while the ambulances and fire engines are allowed to roar through the streets on their sirens.

Many of the picturesque street types have almost vanished in the course of the years, although the rag-and-bone merchant who paid not in cash but in crockery can still be heard calling '*Trapo!*' and the knife grinder, who in the old days used to walk down to Madrid from Orense in Galicia every autumn with his grindstone on his back, announcing his passing with a flute, can still be identified when one hears a flautist in the street. But there are still the merchants of clockwork toys, the black-market tobacco-sellers on the street corners crying *'Tabaco rubio!'* and the sellers of lottery tickets—*'Lotería de mañana!'*

In summer the women water-sellers cry, *'Agua, agua fresca!'*, *'Fresquita la agua!'* or *'Quién querría agua?'* They carry around the water in a porous earthenware *botijo* which keeps it cool by some mysterious process of evaporation; in a tin box at their waist they carry glasses which are scrupulously rinsed after use. Instead of using a glass, you can lift the *botijo* above your head and aim a jet at your mouth. Sooner or later your Spanish friends will try and teach you how to drink wine out of a leather *bota* or a glass *porrón* and the least messy way of learning is to practise first with water. Hold the jar near the neck with the left hand to steady it; the secret lies in the right hand, which is placed at the bottom of the jug and used to tip it up.

Then there are the boot-blacks shouting *'Limpiar!'*. In Spain you only leave your shoes outside your door if you mean them to be thrown away as worn out or useless. If you want them cleaned you go out and have them cleaned on the hoof by a boot-black or *limpiabotas*. These are everywhere and you will find it hard to sit down at a café table without being accosted by one. His legal tariff is three pesetas but you should give him four or five—not more, or you are spoiling the market.

Pay attention or he may try to work the rubber sole trick on you. Tapping your feet to move, he will murmur: *'Sí, Señor?'*, and you, intent on your paper or your conversation, will grunt a *'Sí'* and raise your foot, naturally supposing that shoe to be finished with. Your absentminded grunt, however, has marked the conclusion of a verbal contract, and the next thing you know you have a pair of rubber soles tacked on to your shoes, and the *limpiabotas* is asking you forty-five pesetas for them. Remember that you are quite safe as long as you keep your foot firmly glued to the wooden last; the moment you lift it therefrom your sole is in dire peril!

All Serene!

While not strictly a street cry, one of the commonest cries to be heard in the streets is '*Sereno!*' At intervals during the unquiet Madrid night you may be woken up by shouting, screeching and handclapping in the street and, if you look out of the window, will see an apoplectic gentleman, growing every second angrier, standing and yelling (of all unlikely things): '*Sereno! Sereno!*'

Then you will hear thump-thump on the pavement and a man in a peaked uniform cap will come scurrying up, with a curious dot-and-go-one motion designed to mean that he would break into a canter if it were not for his rheumatics, banging his staff upon

Sereno

the ground as he does so, and will open the front door of one of the houses in order to let in the furibund man, who will give him a peseta tip (unless he wants to be kept waiting even longer next time).

The man with the staff is a famous Madrid character, the *sereno*, whose job it is to guard a number of houses, probably a block or two, and keep their keys from dusk until dawn. He gets his name because, like our watchmen of the eighteenth century (before the weather had gone to the devil like everything else) who used to sing out: 'Four o'clock, a nice clear night and all's well!', he used formerly to call out the hours and to vouchsafe a reassuring prophecy about the morrow's weather—and three hundred and five times out of three hundred and sixty-five (so the modern meteorologists reckon) the old man was right.

He is paid by every user of his doors, who tips him a peseta for letting him in and out each time (but five for a clandestine house of ill-fame), although usually the householders themselves prefer to commute for a flat monthly rate. Although the corps of *serenos* was organised by the Corregidor of Madrid in 1797 and is officially a part of the police, the *sereno* is not paid out of public funds. He is, however, invested with certain legal powers, such as the right of arrest between dusk and dawn, and the right to carry firearms. Occasionally cases appear in the paper where a *sereno* shoots a fleeing burglar, or 'unknown delinquents' kill a *sereno* instead, for the *sereno* has a tradition not only of honesty but of toughness. I have seen a big drunken Murcian who refused to leave a bar in the Barrios Bajos at closing time get a crack over the skull from the *sereno*'s staff which must have lasted him in headaches for some time to come. And quite right too. Big drunken Murcians are bad company anyhow and must be taught manners occasionally.

Over thirteen hundred of these lords of the night hold the keys of Madrid, and nine out of ten of them come from a village called Cangas de Narcea in Asturias. Their staves are made of holly-wood from the great forest of Muniellos, also in Asturias. They have their head-quarters in the Calle de Manzana, and when they retire their Montepío grants them a pension. As a rule the retiring *sereno* sends for a son, a cousin or a nephew from Asturias to replace him, but sometimes a beat in a rich neighbourhood will change hands for a good fat price.

On cold winter nights the *sereno*, who is only human in spite of his curious choice of profession (and will answer to the name of Pepé until you know him better), likes to take shelter in the local tavern, café or some other spot out of the biting wind, and you can get chilled to the liver waiting and yelling for him to let you in. Even worse, however, is having to wait for him to let you out once you are in, for he cannot hear your yells (although everyone else in the house can) nor see you waiting, and it may be a long time before he happens to pass by.

Madrileño architects have a perverse and deplorable passion for stairs; you go into any place—a bar for example—on the ground floor and the restaurant and the lavatory are, nine times out of ten, up or down steep flights of stairs. Even in the American-built Castellana Hilton Hotel you have to go up stairs to get to the main lounge, others to the cloakroom and yet others again to the hairdresser and the lavatory, although all may be said to be on the ground floor. Pandering weakly to this passion for stairs, Madrid lifts, even in newly built blocks, are generally one-way traffic only, taking passengers up but not down. Even if your host offers courteously to come down and let you out, you may have qualms (multiplied according to the note of cold discouragement in his voice) about dragging him down seven flights of draughty stairs in the small hours of the morning when he is obviously longing for his warm bed. Do not be too good a guest, for if he does not walk down with you, you may well be marooned for a quarter of an hour in a dark and viciously draughty passage before the *sereno* comes along. But there is an answer to this problem, as to so many others in Madrid: ask him to give you the house-key; go down and let yourself out; then, leaving the door open, of course (this should be obvious enough, but one can forget that sort of thing in the small hours of the morning), put the key on the floor of the lift and send the lift up again to the seventh floor, leaving him to open the door upstairs and retrieve the key. Of course, this is only practicable if the lift is one of those which have indicator buttons outside, but this at least many Madrid lifts fortunately have, to compensate for their various deficiencies.

To reassure the nervous, who were accustomed to the old three-storey houses, the five-storey houses which came to be built in the last century had—and often still have—the floors called, rather misleadingly, *entresuelo*, *primero*, *principal*, *segundo* and *tercero*. '*Dó*' is short for *derecho* or 'right', and '*izq*' for *izquierdo* or 'left', so that if somebody has the mysterious remark 'Pral dó' on their card it means 'third floor right'.

CHAPTER ELEVEN

The Calle de Alcalá

One of the pleasantest spots to sit of a summer's evening (and one where you can get some of the best draught beer, such as it is) is on the pavement of the Alcalá outside the Cervecería de los Correos just opposite the Post Office. At night Cybele and her lions are lit up, the illuminated fountains play and further on the white and red lights of the cars move up and down the slope of the Alcalá. Floodlights play on the cedar-shaded garden of the Buenavista Palace on the corner, once the home of Goya's Duchess of Alba and of three dictators of Spain, Espartero, Prim and Primo de Rivera.

Two or three hundred yards up the Alcalá the Gran Vía forks off to the right and on the top of the Fénix building, where the two streets join, a nude and boyish figure readily identifiable to any student of classical mythology as Ganymede is being, not very reluctantly, raped by the Eagle and gives a gay, reassuring, bathing-belle kind of wave to a slightly shocked Cybele, sitting sedately in her lion-drawn chariot at the bottom of the street. She, at any rate, she seems to say, knows how to keep her animals in their proper place, little knowing perhaps that those may have been the last words of the Young Lady of Riga.

Madrid is very rich in springs (in 1682 a chronicler

counted seventeen), of which some are left as fountains and others survive only as names. Between them the underground streams and watercourses, the sandy soil and the lack of firm foundations account for the innumerable *socavones* or cave-ins which perpetually disfigure the streets of the city. These *socavones* are supplemented by other holes made by man to irrigate the trees, for we are no longer in the 'treeless, dusty, idle, extortionate Madrid' of Dean Stanley's day. Men with hoses go round all the time washing down the streets, skilfully missing pedestrians and vehicles though laying skid-traps for motor-cyclists, and the streets of the newer quarters are plentifully lined with trees. Most of the streets (and it is one of their chief charms) are built on a very gentle slope, and the trees, like the round pegs they are, are planted in square holes in the concrete which are connected by water channels in the pavement. A hydrant is turned on near the top tree and all the others are irrigated in turn by blocking the channel with mud and then letting the water out to run to the tree below when the higher hole is filled.

What with the irrigation holes and the *socavones* the average Madrileño has learnt not to lift up his eyes to the hills and he limits his range of vision to some five feet nine inches, the distance from the pavement to the head of a pretty girl. This is the more pity because he misses a skyline which Ramón Gómez de la Serna described with his customary understatement as *escafalario* or eccentric.

The roofs are all at different levels. Some loom majestically over fifty miles of the great tableland and from others odd little attics hang askew like bird-cages. Rooftops are capped with turrets, globes, cupolas, crosses, spires and pinnacles, with flimsy Emmet-style erections such as the one on the Bank of Spain or with naked acrobats or fiery steeds prancing eternally on a space of two or three square feet like the talented people who skate on the table tops of nightclubs.

Looking westward up the Alcalá, at its best when silhouetted against the sinking sun, is one of the most extravagant skylines anyone is likely to see this side of New York, for the symptoms of the architectural megalomania which afflict banks and insurance companies in every great city in the world can nowhere be studied to better advantage than in Madrid. Beyond the square tower which flashes an advertisement for Philips Radio rise two enormous bronze quadrigas on the roof of the Banco de Bilbao, hypnotically controlled, in the absence of reins, by naked charioteers in pickelhauben. Below, roosting precariously on the top floor balcony, huge dyspeptic Michelangelesque nudes seem to be complaining sourly to each other about the cold up there.

On the opposite corner of the Calle de Sevilla is the little cast-iron Emmet tower of the Banco Español de Crédito; one's first impression of a howdah appears confirmed by the row of elephants' heads which support this exotic building at the first floor level. Beyond that again, the sky is pierced by the black shape of a gigantic bottle advertising Tio Pepe sherry, dressed up as an Andalusian *caballero* with arms akimbo and, beyond that again, the clock tower of the Gobernación.

One of the finest skyline views of Madrid is to be had from the top of the Calle de Antonio Maura at the corner of the Calle de Alfonso XII, where one can pick out the paralysed chariots on the Banco de Bilbao and a mass of Muscovite spires practically invisible from closer quarters, including a good view of the *embolado* horn which embellishes the Simeón department shop in the Plaza de Santa Ana. As one walks back into the centre, even the chimney cowlings of the Ritz seem to take their place in the fantastic pattern.

The Streets of Madrid

The numbering of streets, like their lighting, their labelling and their cleaning, the collection of refuse, a refuge for mendicants, a fire-service, a savings bank, and many other innovations, was introduced, on the advice of the writer Mesón Romanos, by the enterprising Marqués de Pontejos, the Alcalde who planted out the Castellana. The houses are numbered even on the right and odd on the left starting from the Puerta del Sol end. Streets in London are numbered by the front doors and in Lisbon very often by the ground floor windows, but many of the streets of Madrid are very much longer than they might appear from their numbers owing to the custom of numbering them by properties. This is because the

Pasco de Rosales

building land was sold off by *fincas* or 'lots', each with
its own number, generally two or three to a block which
the Spaniards call by the mysterious name of *manzana* or
'apple'. A typical *finca* in a nineteenth-century street bears
its number over a central front door, which leads to the
flats above, and a couple of shops on either side of it,
so that one number serves where we should use five and
the other end of a long street may be only a few
numbers away.

The Gran Vía

The Gran Vía, otherwise the Avenida de José Antonio,
is a wide modern artery driven through the narrow
twisted streets of the centre. It lies almost exactly athwart
the Puerta del Sol and the numbers start at the junction
with the Alcalá, where Alfonso XIII swung the first
pickaxe in 1910; low numbers such as the Bank of
London and South America and the British-American
Club at No. 6 are at this end and the high numbers
towards the Plaza de España.

The Gran Vía (notice the fantastic fake Gothic building
which is No. 1) illustrates the early twentieth-century
architecture of Madrid better than the Alcalá because
it is less exclusively a creation of bankers. In fact it
provides an important key to the understanding of a
city where, architecturally speaking at least, two wrongs
often make a right and two blacks a white. The general
architectural level of the Gran Vía is not noticeably above
that of Oxford Street; nevertheless the whole effect is
pleasing. I wondered for some time why this should be

so and then realised that the Gran Vía, which would have been a very ugly street were it flat and straight, is redeemed by the fact that it is all on a slope up to the Plaza de Callao and then down again, and that the main or eastern half is set at a gentle curve which is almost exactly the curve of the High at Oxford. One is hardly aware of it, but one cannot see one end from the other.

A second point which I pondered longer was the curiously non-European air of much of the post-Herrera architecture of Madrid such as the so-called neo-baroque of the Post Office and the Telefónica Building. It is certainly not Moorish, for Madrid has been spared the sham-Moorish architecture which has afflicted Andalusia. (The bullring is the only important building in the Mudéjar style.) I thought I hit on one clue from studying the façade of 41 Calle de Alcalá on the corner of the Calle de Valdeiglesias, where the Gran Vía runs into it, for the deeply incised rectangular mouldings casting sharp black shadows on a flat surface surely betray Central American influence. One wonders too whether Pedro Ribera ever saw any Aztec or Maya architecture. His shrines on the Toledo Bridge and the portal of the Hospice would lead one to suspect it.

The other and quite different non-European strain seemed to me, surprisingly enough, Babylonian. It struck me suddenly when I saw an actual truncated pyramid framing an attic window in the Calle de Monte Esquinzo and saw a resemblance to the tapering tower of the Telefónica. But perhaps this is all my fancy, for how Babylonian influences could have reached Madrid I cannot imagine.

The Museum of Drinks

A little way up on the right of the Gran Vía is the famous Chicote Bar, which leads an odd sort of double life. Up to about eight in the evening, it is a respectable bourgeois resort but then, by a sort of tacit and accepted convention, the ladies of good society clear out and the ladies of the town come in and take over. They are (many of them) pretty, well-behaved little creatures who would not dream of speaking until they are spoken to but for whom a meeting of eyes is a meeting of true minds, and a nod or a wink as good as a formal introduction.

In the cellar beneath is a famous and very possibly unique collection of drinks which its owner Perico Chicote has been assembling ever since 1916, when he was barman at the Ritz and the Brazilian Ambassador one day presented him with a bottle of a Brazilian liqueur called *Paraty*. It would not seem to suggest a foundation for a museum to any collector less inveterate than Don José Lázaro-Galdiano, but Don Perico now has some eighteen thousand bottles from about a hundred and fifty countries, including five bottles of 1807 and 1811 Napoleon brandy. There is a complete collection of sherries presented by the bodegas, but otherwise none of the exhibits are of Spanish origin, and all table wines are rigidly excluded except those which are normally asked for in bars, such as champagne. The oldest port bears the date of 1815.

The Museo de Bebidas includes between three and four hundred different whiskies, some of them unique dodo-like examples from long deceased distilleries, about six hundred different rums from the various republics of tropical America, and over two hundred tequilas from Mexico, some a century old. There you will find Philippine rice wine, Danziger Goldwasser with pieces of gold-leaf floating in it, and such exotic beverages as *tedj* from Ethiopia. Liechtenstein makes two contributions, one a wine and the other a kirsch; Andorra is represented by a couple of mountain liqueurs, and Monaco by nine assorted drinks presented by the Prince. There are Liberian rum, gin and port, the last of which bears the encouraging slogan: 'Drink Republic Port, it strengthens the body.' There are yet more dubious potions from Laos, Nepal and Korea, completely unidentifiable behind their hieroglyphics.

The receptacles range from giant and proud Methuselahs to tiny phials which look more suitable for scents or poisons. They are made of glass, china, porcelain, earthenware, crystal and wood. There are coconuts from Brazil and lengths of carved bamboo from the Philippines. The island of Fernando Po contributes a carved and hollowed elephant's tusk, and one 'bottle' containing a Tagalog cocoa spirit is even made of straw.

The shapes of these receptacles are as fantastically varied as the materials. There is hardly an animal in zoology whose likeness has not been blown, cast, moulded or carved to hold some liqueur or other. Music and the theatre, architecture and religion, have all been pressed into service. There are the inevitable bottles with built-in musical boxes from Switzerland and Germany, and an Italian one with puppets which perform when it is tilted. A *grappa* comes in a miniature Leaning Tower of

Pisa, possibly to demonstrate its effectiveness upon the human equilibrium, and a Calvados in the Cathedral not of Lisieux but of Lourdes. The Mexicans produce tequila bottles in the shape of the Virgin of Guadalupe and one of them even has a coloured image of her inside, well pickled over the years in the fiery spirit of her country.

The Gay Centre

The Gran Vía is now the principal shopping street of Madrid and consequently the most crowded. There and in the section of the Calle de Alcalá adjoining are some of the most expensive shops for jewellery, haberdashery, leather goods and so forth. Further up is the local Woolworth's called Sepu and on the pencil-slim corner of the Plaza de Callao and the Calle de los Preciados rises the sixteen-storey department store, the Galerías Preciados. The Calle de los Peligros, which runs from the Gran Vía to the Alcalá contains some high-class food shops, while the Calle de Fuencarral seems to run mainly to shoe shops.

The part of the street on both sides of the Plaza de Callao is the centre for the fixed-session or first-showing cinemas. There are about thirty of these in Madrid, whose performances take place usually at seven and eleven o'clock, but in any case are advertised in the papers. The remaining cinemas have continuous showings, some starting in the morning and others in the afternoon. (Give a peseta to the attendant who shows you to your seat.) Almost all foreign films are dubbed into Spanish and the only cinema which used to show foreign films in the original recently switched to Spanish.

There are two good bookshops in the Gran Vía, the Casa del Libro of the Espasa-Calpe publishing house and the Librería Franco-Española; there are others in the Calle de los Preciados and in the Puerta del Sol such as Fernando Fé. All these carry English books, but perhaps the widest selection of all is to be found at Buchholtz in the Paseo de los Recoletos.

The Life of the Streets

The *paseo* in Madrid is no longer what it was. In its original form of groups of young men in twos and threes and groups of young women in twos and threes parading at a given hour of the evening in opposite directions to each other and flirting discreetly across the invisible central barrier of a recognised *paseo*, *avenida* or street it survives only in the provinces. But still of an evening you will find the Gran Vía filled with people, some on their way to the cinemas, shops or cafés but many aimlessly parading, the women mostly looking trim and well-dressed in their Sunday best. Not all the Spaniards are good-looking by any means but you will hardly see a face which has not the marks of a strongly individual personality stamped upon it. There are few of the pie-faced, poe-faced types so common among the visitors from Northern Europe and North America. There is a high standard of female beauty in Madrid, but even those women who are not strictly beautiful are usually attractive with their fine eyes, small feet, and beautiful rich black hair—which exercises what scientists call capillary attraction.

Black is perhaps the commonest colour worn until the spring sun brings out gayer hues, no doubt partly because of the seriousness with which mourning is taken and partly because the women know it suits them. For Mass they wear little black veils on their heads. To see the smartest clothes of the women, watch them coming out of Sunday Mass at such fashionable churches as the Medinaceli, or San José and the Calatravas in the Alcalá, or in the case of the more mature ladies of Society at the charity bridge and canasta tournaments at the Castellana Hilton, which punctuate their lives in the winter.

Manners and Modes

Spain is a good deal more formal than France or Italy, if not in modes of address, at least as far as dress is concerned. Even in high summer men's jackets may not be taken off indoors. They are a symbol of respectability like lace curtains, a flag which must not be struck. If you come coatless into a café, restaurant or cinema you may be asked to put your jacket on or to leave. There is more sense in this than might at first appear, for stepping out from the hot sunshine into a cool, shaded interior such as a church may easily mean a drop of ten or fifteen degrees in the temperature.

Shorts for men and slacks for women are looked on askance except at the seaside. In a word you should dress as for a city and not as if you were in the Salzkammergut. But even here American influence is making headway and not so long ago a Spanish journalist rather sourly wrote that in Madrid they were getting accustomed to seeing their best hotels occupied to all appearance by mechanics and artisans. There is something to be said for the maintenance of conventional standards and still more in favour of observing the prejudices of the people among whom you are a guest, but one cannot fail to observe that the opposition in the foreign colony to open shirts and no coats seems to stem mainly from women who can freely wear cotton dresses and from the business men, diplomats and teachers who have to wear coats, collars and ties for professional reasons.

The typical Spanish costumes themselves are seldom to be seen nowadays in Madrid. Cloaks cost three thousand five hundred or four thousand pesetas and, although a few appear in the winter, they are mostly worn by men who have obviously had them for many years or have inherited them; the flat stiff wide-brimmed Cordoba hats are only worn for riding or by old bullfighters; shawls, mantillas and high combs are no longer seen even at the *toros*, although thousands of fans wave like foxhounds' sterns ceaselessly on hot afternoons. At the principal *corrida* at the Seville Fair, the greatest stronghold of tradition in Spain, I counted only fourteen mantillas in the whole bullring.

The rules about dress in church are strict. Men must wear long trousers, a closed collar and a coat which covers the arms; women may not wear slacks and must cover their heads even if only with a handkerchief. Cardinal Pla's 'Code of Feminine Morality' lays down the following rules for visitors to churches. Clothing must not reveal the body in a 'provocative' manner, skirts must cover the legs to below the knee and sleeves the arms to below the elbow, these two being evidently among the more highly 'provocative' joints. Plunging necklines are gravely sinful. Stockings must be worn. Even children's thighs must be covered. So now the tourist has been warned.

Masculine manners have undergone a great improvement during the time I have known Spain. The old habits of spitting and bottom-pinching have joined the gutting of horses in the bullring as disagreeable memories of the past. But one thing any pretty girl on her own must be prepared for in the streets is the *piropo* or compliment, the tribute which gallant males feel impelled to pay to beauty as it passes. And beauty passes. It is an old Spanish custom and no action or reply is called for. Only if the *caballero* gets too persuasive or rude does he pass the line which divides him from a *gamberro* or hooligan who deserves the attentions of the police.

Hotels

Several of the *lujo* hotels and many of the cheaper categories, *residencias* and pensions are here in the Gran Vía. Hotels in Spain are strictly controlled both as to quality and to price by the Dirección General de Turismo, an organisation set up by the Government to foster and protect what has in recent years become Spain's largest earner of foreign currency. They are divided into five categories: *lujo* or luxury which can be pretty expensive, especially if you have a lot of extras, 1A, 1B, 2 and 3. The last four categories, at any rate, have their prices strictly controlled and give very good value for money. (I lived for two years in a penthouse suite in a category 1A hotel in the centre of the city for about £1 a day, which covered bedroom, sitting-room, bathroom and terrace, light, heat and telephone.)

One may wonder how these divisions are made, for clearly conditions keep on changing all the time and no two people would agree upon the precise merits of a hotel, one man preferring sound plumbing, another a good cuisine and yet a third a friendly, welcoming atmosphere, although that, to be sure, is seldom lacking in a Spanish hotel. So the categories are divided according to the arbitrary yardstick of the proportion of bathrooms to rooms or to floors. In parenthesis, the Spanish preference for douches (there is generally at least a hot and cold shower-bath in your room) may perhaps be traced to the very logical Arab view that one should always wash in running water, for if you bathe or wash in stagnant water you merely get your own dirt back again.

Remember when filling up forms that your name or *nombre* is your Christian name and that your surname is your appellation or *apelido*. Spanish names are to a considerable extent a matter of the personal taste of their owner. Thus a man generally adds his mother's maiden name to his father's surname. As Archibald Laurence Lyall I usually find myself entered in hotels as Mr. Laurence, Lyall being assumed to be the name of my mother. In 1931 I got into trouble in the Rif on suspicion of being 'the notorious Colonel Lawrence'!

If your father's name was Smith and your mother's Jones you have the choice of calling yourself Mr. Smith, Mr. Smith Jones, Mr. Smith y Jones, or even if you like, just Mr. Jones. (Velázquez was the name of the painter's mother; his father was called de Silva.) Noblemen often use their family names in preference to their title, and married women, in a country where they have no right even to their own private estate, frequently retain and use their maiden names right up to the time their obituary notices appear. Out of all this confusion the sole beneficiary is the itinerant adulterer, since no hotel clerk can tell by looking at their papers whether his guests are man and wife or not.

The Water

The crack of an English wit to the effect that 'the pain in Spain stems mainly from the drains' is not really justified, but at least one problem which always confronts the traveller in a strange land may be worth a solvent paragraph. A 'Gents' is usually labelled '*Caballeros*' (how wonderful to be in a country where everyone is a knight just by virtue of his sex!) and a 'Ladies' is '*Señoras*', but prudishness about marking lavatories for everyone to see often makes for embarrassment when foreign ladies with no knowledge of the language have to hunt for someone to ask the way from. Often you dive through a very promising door, only to find yourself in a kitchen or a pantry and having to ask the way from the scullions. Where lavatories in hotels and restaurants are labelled, they bear a bewildering variety of names such as *Servicios*—you ask the waiter for *los servicios* or for the Anglo-Spanish *el vater*, the English w.c. (*Water Caballeros* always conjures up to me rococo visions of knights on seahorses caracoling to water music); a *retrete*, which means 'retreat'—the Italian *ritirata;* a *lavabo*—Latin for 'I will wash' (but with the plural *lavabos*, not *lavabimus*); an *aseo*—literally 'cleanliness'; a *tocador de señoras*, which is not a gentleman who likes touching ladies, but a 'ladies' touching up place'; or even (this rare specimen I found in the Madrid Zoo) the magniloquent *evacuatorio*. Sometimes, rather whimsically, it is labelled '*Por Aquí*' or '*Aquí Está*'.

It is as well to bring out a roll of English lavatory paper and carry some round in your pocket. The Spanish are often said to be very thin-skinned, but this accusation is to be taken in a purely metaphorical sense.

The Soho of Madrid

To the north of the Gran Vía is a district of bars, night-clubs and small restaurants. *Tascas* where one can eat well and cheaply in the streets behind Chicote's are Los Siete Picos in the Calle de las Infantes, Las Vascongadas in the Plaza de Vasquez Mella, Arrumbumbaya in the Calle de la Libertad, Salvador in the Calle de Barbieri and the Argentina on the corner of the Calle de Gravina and the Calle de Valgamedíos.

Further up behind the Telefónica, in a district marked by a number of rather dubious bars, are many others such as the Restaurant de Trabuco, the Restaurant de la Prensa, the Gran Taverna and the Gran Tasca. More exotic restaurants in this district are the China Restaurant in the Calle de Valverde, where the portions of Chow Mien and Sweet-and-Sour are so large that you should go with a friend to do justice to them, the Italian Osteria Serenella in the Calle de Jiménez Quesada, and the Bósforo in the

Calle de la Concepción de Arenal, which specialises in Hungarian and Oriental dishes. Down in the Calle de San Leonardo, behind the Edificio España, is a Mexican restaurant called El Charro. On the other side of the Gran Vía in the Calle de los Jardines is a South American restaurant called El Rancho de Tranquilino, Chilean-owned, Hungarian-managed but Argentine-style, which is famous for its meat. Also on the other side of the Gran Vía is a *tasca* which should not be missed by the amateur of local colour. El Callejón, where a good many theatre people go, is a *tasca* on the typical old Madrid plan with a bar in front and three or four connecting rooms behind. It has a special *plat du jour* featuring some local dish every day of the week. Thus Monday—*cocido madrileño*; Tuesday—*fabada asturiana*; Friday—*bacalao a la vizcaina* and so forth. It is good too for such dishes as *angulas* and prawns cooked in garlic. The Callejón is not easy to find. It is in the Calle de Ternera, a narrow lane which runs off the Calle de los Preciados nearly opposite the Korynto Restaurant.

CHAPTER TWELVE

The Old University Quarter

Past the Plaza de Callao, where it dips down the hill towards the Plaza de España, the Gran Vía cuts through the San Bernardo Quarter, mostly built in the early eighteenth century, when the florid Spanish baroque style known as Churriguerresque had come into fashion.

The reign of Philip II was distinguished by the austere, 'unornamented' style of Juan de Herrera, the architect of the Escorial. Of his surviving work in Madrid itself, perhaps the most attractive is the Segovia Bridge of 1584 (which does not lead to Segovia at all but to Estremadura). Only a shade less severe were the architects of Philip III and Philip IV, but the wheel turns full circle with the reign of Charles II and the riotous style of Churriguerra, whose local apostle in Madrid was the *Maestro de Obras*, Pedro de Rivera, the pupil who outdid his master. In 1732, he designed the Toledo Bridge with its richly carved shrines of St. Isidore and his wife, which contrast so strongly with the plainness of Herrera's bridge, decorated only by the granite globes which were his trademark. But the principal examples of Ribera's work are the Statue of Fame in the Calle de Barceló and the flamboyant Churriguerresque portals in the San

Bernardo Quarter. They may be seen at the Conde-Duque barracks and the Church of the Benedictines in the Calle de Montserrat, but the most extravagant and typical of all is that of the Municipal Hospice, now the Municipal Museum, in the Calle de Fuencarral.

This little visited museum contains an interesting historical collection of maps, prints and engravings of the city. Some of the most surprising show the Manzanares full of water from one end of the long Segovia Bridge to the other with boats sailing up and down it. There are fine examples of ceramics from the old Retiro factory destroyed by the French and there is the original Maria-blanca, an ancient statue of Venus or Diana, which for centuries presided over the fountain in the Puerta del Sol and even became the patroness of the water-carriers because the people took it for the Virgin Mary.

On the whole the streets of the San Bernardo Quarter are shoddy and narrow and its principal distinction is that it has been the University Quarter since 1823, when the sixteenth-century university of Alcalá de Henares was moved to the old Jesuit Novitiate in the Calle de San Bernardo.

Up to 1834 the little town of Alcalá de Henares on the road to Guadalajara ('Don John of Austria is gone by Alcalá') boasted thirty-eight churches, twenty-one convents and twenty-seven religious colleges. Now bored and sloppy sentries lounge in front of the doors of the old buildings, which have mostly been turned into barracks, prisons and reformatories. The pigeons wheel round the ragged storks' nests on the towers of the deserted convents. Higher against the blue sky glide the hopeful hawks and immensely far above them again roar the jet fighters from the air base at Torrejón. How pleasant, one sometimes thinks, it would be if the University could be moved back to give life again to the empty cobbled streets and forsaken colleges of this little failed Oxford. But that is impossible. Madrid has long outgrown Alcalá. Most of the students live at home or in lodgings, and a University must be in or close to a city. So the third site in less than a century and a half is to be the University City now being built on the north-western edge of Madrid.

The quarter retains a faintly academic atmosphere, and the Calle de Los Libreros, which still contains half a dozen secondhand bookshops, bears one of the very few Madrid street names of the sort, Curtidores, Herradores, Tintoreros, Bordaderos, and so forth, which retain any connection with their original trades, although there is still one solitary cutler left in the Calle de los Cuchilleros. But even in its own field the Calle de los Libreros is left behind, for the main secondhand book market, founded forty or fifty years ago, is down at Atocha in the Calle de Claudio Moyano, where twenty-seven stalls back up against the railings of the Botanical Gardens.

Perhaps the most interesting place in the quarter is the Romantic Museum in the Calle de San Mateo, to which I know no exact equivalent in Europe. It is the embodiment of everything that is *castizo*, a practically untranslatable Castilian word meaning typical, unspoilt, pure of lineage, in the tradition. An aristocratic house built about 1840, it was furnished by its owner, the connoisseur Marqués de Vega-Inclán with period pictures by such painters as Madrazo and Vicente López, furniture, porcelain, carpets, curtains, ornaments and sculpture of the period which we should call Early Victorian and the Spaniards call Romantic. It takes its name from the Romantic Movement which after the success of Victor Hugo's *Hernani* spread like a forest fire across the Pyrenees and in Spain transformed not only painting and the theatre but interior decoration, furniture, clothes, and taste and fashion generally, especially after 1835 when the Duke of Rivas staged his play, *Don Alvaro: o La Fuerza del Sino*. Two curious contemporary pieces brought here are the pistols with which the famous poet and dandy Mariano de Larra shot himself in the crypt of the church of Santa Clara, and the more than sumptuous privy of Ferdinand VII. There are remarkable examples of the minor decorative arts peculiar to the period such as bouquets and suchlike ingenious confections made of seashells.

By a curious coincidence, Madrid and its neighbourhood have two other period-furnished houses, one about fifty years later and one about fifty years earlier. The Museo de Cerralbo in the Calle de Ventura Rodríguez shows how heavy and fussy the furnishings and interior of a nobleman's house have become by the end of the century. The Casa del Labrador at Aranjuez, on the other hand (Labrador here, as in the case of St. Isidore, means a farm labourer and not a dog), is a Spanish version of the Petit Trianon. As at Versailles, the eighteenth-century notion of the simple life, in very marked contrast to that of Philip II, implied a reduction in size only and not in luxury, in quantity and not in quality. Only one small room on the ground floor mimics a peasant's hovel, its walls cunningly painted to resemble peeling stucco with the brickwork showing through. The rest of the Casita is perhaps the most nearly perfect example of a furnished *Empire* house in existence. Built in 1803, it has hardly been lived in at all, for the Bourbon Monarchy fell five years later and the house was never occupied again. The *Empire* furnishings and decorations are absolutely untouched—in what stamp-dealers would call 'mint condition'—exactly as when they were installed for Charles IV. There is even an *Empire* billiard room with an *Empire* billiard table with *Empire* legs and *Empire* cues of ebony inlaid with gold and silver with ivory tips.

The Plaza de España

The Gran Vía runs down into the large Plaza de España on to which face two new skyscrapers, the Torre de Madrid and the Edificio España. Comparisons are often as interesting as they are odious, and some rather illuminating ones may be drawn between the Escorial, which is three-quarters of a mile round, and the twenty-eight-storey Edificio España. On an area hardly larger than one of the Escorial's sixteen courtyards the latter has three thousand one hundred and twenty-three windows to the Escorial's two thousand seven hundred and eleven, but four thousand one hundred and forty-six doors to the Escorial's mere one thousand two hundred. From the great rooms of the sixteenth-century monastery-palace-pantheon to the little intercommunicating hutches of a modern office block!

From here the wide Calle de la Princesa (the Princess was the greatly loved *La Chata* or 'Snubnose', the sister of King Alfonso XII) runs up north-west to Moncloa, the University City and, if you care to go on far enough, to the sea at La Coruña.

The Palacio de Liria

Lying in cedar-shaded gardens a little back from the Calle de la Princesa is the finest private palace in Madrid, Ventura Rodríguez's Palacio de Liria, which belongs to the Duke and Duchess of Alba. The great staircase was famed for its fine Mudéjar ceiling, brought by a Duke of Alba from his Miranda Palace at Peñaranda de Duero, but this was destroyed when the Palace was burnt out in the revolution of 1936. Now the Albas have restored the Palace and live in it. They readily grant permission (to be asked for by letter) to go over the Palace and to visit the historic treasures which must be well-nigh unrivalled for a private collection.

There are many relics of the Empress Eugénie of France, whose sister Francisca married the fifteenth Duke and who lived at one time in the Palace, and a number of Stuart portraits ranging from Mary, Queen of Scots to the Cardinal of York, for Royal Stuart blood runs in the Alba veins and they number the Dukedom of Berwick among their titles. James Fitzjames Stuart, first Duke of Berwick, was an illegitimate son of James II and Arabella Churchill, sister of the great Duke of Marlborough. The natural son of an English king became a naturalised Frenchman, a Marshal of France and Commander-in-Chief of the armies of Philip V, who created him Duke of Liria for his services in conquering Spain for the Bourbons. The third Duke of Berwick and

Liria married the twelfth Duchess of Alba in her own right and the present Alba family stems from the union. Habsburgwise the Albas married into many great families and inherited such valuable heirlooms as the Conde-Duque's collection of pictures and many later works of art from the Montijo family.

The historic documents include letters from Henry VIII of England and some rather acid complaints from Queen Elizabeth to the 'great' Duke of Alba, Regent of the Netherlands, about his treatment of some English merchants at Bergen-op-Zoom. There are letters of Ferdinand and Isabella and their original will signed, as was the custom, *Yo El Rey* and *Yo La Reina*. There are letters from Columbus signed *El Almirante* and his logbook with the first map he made of Santo Domingo. (Perhaps the most curious Columbus relic in Spain hangs in the north transept of Burgos Cathedral—the rusty bird-cage in which he brought the first tropical birds from the New World.) There are the will of Philip II and the original Bull of Pope Alexander VI granting the Indies to Spain. Among the paintings are works by Titian, Bellini and Goya, Fra Angelico's lovely *Madonna with the Pomegranate* and Rubens' copy of Titian's lost portrait of Charles V and his wife Isabel.

The Calle de la Princesa

This rather bloodstained north-western suburb of Madrid is called Argüelles, and parallel with the Calle de la Princesa to the west is the smart new Paseo de Rosales, built on what was once the Montaña de Principe Pio, the scene alike of the shootings of May 3rd, 1808, painted by Goya and of the abortive revolt of General Fanjul and the garrison of the Montaña Barracks in July 1936. At the end of the Calle de la Princesa is the Plaza de Moncloa, where on summer evenings the poor come to catch the breeze from the Sierra and to eat their supper in the *merenderos* to the music of the barrel organs. All this part of Madrid was flattened in the Civil War and on the left of the Plaza is the enormous Air Ministry recently built on the site of the Model Prison where the Reds executed many prisoners in October 1936. It is built in the *desorna-mentado* 'Second Renaissance' style and its resemblance to a slightly shrunken Escorial caused the local wits to christen it 'the Air Monastery'.

A little further on is a triumphal arch which makes a noble entry into Madrid. But Madrid is singularly fortunate in all its road entries, at least from the north— from what the Spaniards themselves call 'Europe'. From La Coruña and Segovia the arriving visitor drives along a two-track road bordered for about ten miles by ole-anders and other flowering shrubs through the young woodlands of the University City and down the broad Calle de la Princesa, across the Plaza de España, and straight into the Gran Vía. Coming from Burgos and San Sebastian, he comes suddenly into the Avenida del Generalísimo and straight down the lovely Castellana. The road from Barcelona somehow manages to by-pass the slums of the Carretera de Aragón and turn into the shrub-bordered road from Barajas Airport, debouching into the Castellana almost opposite the Hilton Hotel. Even the Estremadura Highway has the impressive view of the Pasco de Rosales, a line of apartment blocks broken at intervals by small skyscrapers on the high bluff above the Manzanares so that Madrid looks from below like a walled and towered hilltop city. Only coming in from Valencia and Andalusia does one have to pass through the sordid outskirts common to all great cities.

The University City

If the Escorial was the great dream of Philip II, the University was that of Alfonso XIII by which he wished his reign to go down to posterity. Colleges, lecture halls, libraries, hostels, clinics and hospitals sprung up in the rolling country outside the Puerta de Hierro and as each was finished in turn the faculties began to move out from their cramped quarters in San Bernardo. It is ironic to think that the royal begetter of this far-sighted and imaginative scheme was hardly ever allowed by his advisers to visit it and watch its progress for fear of demonstrations and insults, for the students who were to benefit from it were republicans almost to a man.

Then from 1936 to 1939 it was the most stubbornly contested battlefield of the Civil War, being the solitary Nationalist foothold on the left bank of the Manzanares. Everything in it was destroyed and after the war the City had to be built for the second time in twenty years. Soon it will be completed and the whole University will be moved out there. Like most of those in modern Madrid, the buildings are all of brick and limestone and, if their creators can be said to have drawn any inspiration from the capital at all, it would fortunately seem to be from the architect of the chaste neoclassical Palacio Buenavista rather than the gloomy puritanical Herrera or the exuberant vulgarians at the Calle de Alcalá. Only a tenth of the land is to be built over and the rest is being preserved as open space, most of which has been planted with pines, poplars and flowering acacias. When they have grown up, the University City should be a forest with lawns and glades and buildings scattered through it. It is certainly an essential excursion for visiting townplanners, architects and educationalists.

Beyond the Iron Gate

To the east of the University City is the latest settlement of the Madrid millionaires, the luxurious and daily growing garden city of La Ciudad de la Puerta de Hierro. Beyond, on the Coruña road, are their favourite playgrounds, the country clubs of Puerta de Hierro and the Club de Campo with golf courses, polo grounds, tennis courts and swimming pools. Further out still is the Playa de Madrid where the Manzanares has been dammed to form a lake and a public swimming pool. (Other public swimming pools are the Stella, where the Calle de López de Hoyos crosses the Ciudad Lineal, El Lago in the Paseo de Florida, and the Piscina Municipal in the Casa del Campo, besides various private clubs.)

Plaza de la Cebada

Beyond the Playa de Madrid, at the Hill of Partridges, on the right of the Coruña road, is the racecourse, the Hipódromo de la Zarzuela, which is said to be the only racecourse in the world where you can sit down at a table over your drinks actually at the winning post.

Restaurants, roadhouses, nightclubs, swimming pools, villas and chalets stretch out halfway along the road to the Escorial and make it virtually a suburb of Madrid. (It is disillusioning to learn that one of the most euphonious names in the Gazetteer means literally 'a slagheap', for the little town occupies the site of a Roman mining village called Scoriae.) A number of summer chalets and villas now cluster above Philip II's gigantic and rather sinister Monastery-Palace-Pantheon, possibly the largest man-made accumulation of stone blocks after the Pyramids.

Steeply behind the Escorial rise the heights of the Sierra de Guadarrama, whither young Madrileños flock out from the Estación del Norte with skis over their shoulders at winter week-ends and over which the high passes lead to Segovia, Avila and the ancient cities of Old Castile.